The latest

Ninja Foodi PossibleCooker

Cookbook for Beginners

Enjoy Your Favorite Dishes with Plenty of Mouthwatering Ninja Foodi PossibleCooker Recipes and Beginner-Friendly Instructions

Betty Lacourse

Table of Contents

Introduction

Cooking is a great art with a secret language that we find interesting to share. This book will show a new innovation that can become your best kitchen companion, the Ninja Foodi PossibleCooker. You need to master the secrets of this appliance to be sure you will get an amazing dance of flavors.

This appliance will allow you to cook endless amazing meals, from roasts to crispy casseroles. It is a game-changer that combines the functionalities of a slow cooker, bake oven, frying pan and more, all bundled in one sleek device. It goes beyond being a mere device and promises to be your kitchen friend to transform your general experience.

Once you acquire the device, you are assured of several benefits. You get quality assurance, value for your money, performance is awesome, it has a nice appearance, you enjoy its versatility, and it is easy to use and clean. Thus, the Ninja Foodi PossibleCooker brings efficiency.

This book will highlight several essentials, including:
• The basic fundamentals of Ninja Foodi PossibleCooker
• The advantages you will get as you use the appliance
• Get an inside overview of its accessories.
• You will get a guide when acquiring it from the store.
• Maintenance is a good consideration when you need your gadget to stay longer. Thus, you get tips on cleaning and
• caring for the appliance.
• You will also get some frequently asked questions and other notes on the usage.

This cookbook is a wonderful guide. It goes beyond being a collection of recipes; it will unlock your kitchen's full potential, and you will enjoy one amazing and delicious dish at a time. Let's explore its possibilities.

Fundamentals of Ninja Foodi PossibleCooker

Do you know a kitchen appliance that promises to transform your cooking experience? Ninja Foodi PossibleCooker is here to assure you of the best experience, and you will understand the fundamentals before using the gadget. You might have seen the appliance in your friend's kitchen, heard more about it across the social media buzz, or seen it in the local appliance store you visited recently. Your curiosity might have heightened, and you need it in your kitchen.

From a mere glance, you may take this as another common kitchen device. But you won't believe it; the Ninja Foodi PossibleCooker is a versatile kitchen appliance with a unique design that simplifies your kitchen adventure. Instead of wondering where you heard it from, take it in your kitchen and prepare those delicious recipes you always see online from your favorite chefs or cooking shows.

The sleek design and ability to slow cook, bake, steam, sear/sauté and other cooking tasks packaged in one appliance unifies this device. If you watched these capabilities on a cooking show or read a food blog, now is the time to bring it to your kitchen.

As we explore the fundamentals, take this gadget as your gate pass to the wonders of the culinary world. Unlock the full potential of this device by understanding the basics, whether you are a beginner or a seasoned chef. Enjoy the cooking and make it a wonderful experience.

What is Ninja Foodi PossibleCooker?

There are many kitchen appliances in the market. As a brand, Ninja ensures that every kitchen gets the best in terms of simplicity, space utilization, and technology adoption. Both seasoned chefs and new cooks have a unique way to benefit from the Ninja Foodi PossibleCooker. We ask ourselves, 'What is Ninja Foodi PossibleCooker, and how does it redefine the cooking adventure?'

The Ninja Foodi PossibleCooker is a multifunctional device that seamlessly integrates several cooking methods. You can think of it as a sleek and efficient kitchen appliance that combines the functionalities of a bake oven, a crockpot, a frying pan, and much more – all within one single device. The appliance brings the best cooking experience, where you can achieve an array of cooking tasks without much stress.

Everyone is talking about the versatility of this gadget. Both traditional kitchens and contemporary cooking spaces are ready to grab all the benefits of this appliance. The multifaceted capabilities make a nice go-to appliance. And what makes it win against other appliances is the ability to seamlessly transition between the various cooking functions. It can easily adapt to different functions, making it a unique kitchen gadget to buy, especially with modern cooking where most people are busy. You will enjoy your home cooking and take it to newer heights.

Join this era of cooking with this appliance and convert your kitchen into a hub of creativity and flavor. Seamlessly converge efficiency, versatility, and kitchen innovation. Are you ready to unlock the door that introduces you to the world of many possibilities within the kitchen?

Benefits of Using It

The Ninja Foodi PossibleCooker is here as a wonderful gadget revolutionizing how you do your cooking. It has taken into account the changing dynamics of technology, promising unique features to enhance your experience. You will get lots of benefits when you decide to use this appliance. Some of the benefits are:

1. You Will Enjoy Redefined Versatility:
The Ninja Foodi PossibleCooker is an appliance that can serve you in multiple ways and guarantees a seamless transition from one cooking function to another. Do you want to grill? The gadget will serve you. You can also bake, sear/sauté, sous vide, do your proofing, steaming, braising, slow cooking, and much more. All these functions are contained in one simple package. Such versatility gives you the ample calmness of enjoying a variety of recipes without needing multiple gadgets.

2. Time-Efficient Cooking:
Modern life has made many people busy, and time has become a very important factor to consider. Whenever you need to do your quick and efficient cooking, the Ninja Foodi PossibleCooker comes to your rescue. You can prepare your food faster as compared to the traditional methods. Busy families or individuals have a reason to smile.

3. Consistent and Precise Results:

When using some other appliances or the traditional ways, you may have cycles where one day everything is perfect; then the next day turns out awkward. The Ninja Foodi PossibleCooker guarantees consistency in your everyday cooking. You have precise temperature control and cooking modes, ensuring each dish is perfectly cooked. You could prepare a flavorful beef stew and chicken casserole.

4. Reduction in Kitchen Clutter:

Your countertops won't be cluttered. No more overstuffing of your cabinets. Since the Ninja Foodi PossibleCooker comes as a multifunctional device, there is no need for multiple appliances. This is a good way to streamline the space within your kitchen. And since it comprises the functions of many devices, you save in both space and the hassle of using different appliances.

5. Unleashed the Kitchen Creativity:

This is the best moment to go to your kitchen and experiment with different recipes. Make sure you try out the different functions, giving you an opportunity to see the different kitchen possibilities and come up with new recipes, cooking methods, and amazing flavors. You can try gourmet meals, sides, seafood, and the irresistible snacks.

6. Safe and Easy-to-Use Interface:

It is a user-friendly gadget free of cadmium, lead, and PFOA. The Ninja Foodi PossibleCooker has an intuitive interface, and you can easily navigate the settings. The design of the controls is easy for anyone to use, from tech-savvy individuals to those who are starting their cooking adventure.

7. Energy Efficiency:

Energy conservation has become a necessity in the current world. The design of the Ninja Foodi PossibleCooker focuses on efficiency. Given that it can perform multiple cooking functions, it minimizes the need for additional appliances, making your kitchen more energy-efficient.

8. Easy Cleanup:

The happiness of your cooking process is on top level whenever you have less cleaning to do. Ninja Foodi PossibleCooker is good at that to give you peace of mind after enjoying your delicious meal. It has removable, dishwasher-safe components that make cleaning very easy. The pot is nonstick, allowing you to easily wipe out any messes.

9. Enhances Flavor and Texture:

You will realize that your meals' flavor and texture improve when you use the Ninja Foodi PossibleCooker. Every dish is unique. Sit down and bring out a perfect sear on your steak. Your roast will have that succulent juiciness.

Setting up before the first time:

First, unbox the main unit by unwrapping and removing all the packaging material, stickers or labels, and tapes attached to the unit.

Unbox and remove all the accessories that come with the unit from the package, ensuring you carefully review the manual. Focusing on the dos and don'ts is advisable to ensure everything goes smoothly. Check closely on the warnings, operational instructions, and essential safeguards to ensure no property damage or injury occurs.

Next, ensure the main base unit, the inner cooking pot, the spoon-ladle, and the lid get a good wash using a clean, damp, soapy towel. Warm water with a bit of soap does the trick. Do not try to immerse the main unit in water.

After washing, rinse them well and pat dry or air dry before the next cooking phase or before storing. If you're not up for hand washing, most parts are also okay to pop in the dishwasher.

Before you use the appliance, you need to turn it on and allow it to run for 10 minutes before adding any ingredient. Your kitchen needs to be well-ventilated. It is a good consideration to do away with any residual packaging substances and remaining odors. This step is safe and won't interfere with the performance of your gadget.

Slow Cook Function

1. Open the lid. Always ensure your hands are dry.
2. Plug in the Ninja Foodi PossibleCooker.
3. Place the cooking pot inside the unit. Ensure the pot's indent lines up with the rear bump of the main unit.
4. Confirm all the accessories are in place.
5. Turn on the device using the power button.
6. Turn the dial to choose the SLOW COOK function.
7. Utilize the +/- TEMP arrows to adjust your temperature by picking either HI or LO temperature settings.
8. Set your appropriate cooking time according to your recipe between 3 and 12 hours, adjusting in 15-minute intervals.
   Note: you can easily adjust SLOW COOK LO time between 6 and 12 hours, and SLOW COOK HI may stand between 3 and 12 hours.
9. Press START/STOP button to initiate the cooking process.
10. Add in your ingredients and close the lid.
11. Once the cooking time elapses, you will hear a beep from the unit, and it will automatically transition to the KEEP WARM mode while counting up.

Seer/Saute Function

1. Open the lid. Always ensure your hands are dry.
2. Plug in the Ninja Foodi PossibleCooker.

3. Place the cooking pot inside the unit. Ensure the pot's indent lines up with the rear bump of the main unit.
4. Confirm all the accessories are in place.
5. Turn on the device using the power button.
6. Turn the dial to choose the SEAR/SAUTE function.
7. Utilize the +/- TEMP arrows to adjust your temperature by picking either HI or LO temperature settings.
8. Now, set your appropriate cooking duration according to your recipe. Using the arrow buttons, you can increase or decrease the time by intervals of one minute, going up to 15 minutes.
9. Ready to preheat? Press the start button. The screen will display 'PRE,' and a progress bar will show the progress. This process might take around 5 minutes but varies based on your chosen temperature.
10. Once preheated, you'll hear a beep; it is time to add your ingredients.
11. Lift the lid and arrange your food inside the cooking pot. Shut the lid, and your cooking starts with the timer ticking away.
12. You can press START/STOP button to stop the sear/sauté process.

Steam Function
1. Open the lid. Always ensure your hands are dry.
2. Plug in the Ninja Foodi PossibleCooker.
3. Place the cooking pot inside the unit. Ensure the pot's indent lines up with the rear bump of the main unit.
4. Confirm all the accessories are in place.
5. Turn on the device using the power button.
6. Turn the dial to choose the STEAM function.
7. Utilize the +/- TEMP arrows to adjust the temperature.
8. Now, set your appropriate cooking duration according to your recipe. You can increase or decrease the time by one minute intervals using the arrow buttons.
9. Ready to preheat? Press the start/stop button. The screen will display 'PRE,' and a progress bar will show the progress. This process might take around 5 minutes but varies based on your chosen temperature.
10. Lift the lid and arrange your food inside the cooking pot. Shut the lid, and your cooking starts with the timer ticking away.
11. Once the cooking time elapses, you will hear a beep from the unit, and the unit displays END.
   Note: The unit automatically transitions to the KEEP WARM function when coming to the end of each cooking cycle.

Keep Warm Function

1. Open the lid. Always ensure your hands are dry.
2. Plug in the Ninja Foodi PossibleCooker.
3. Place the cooking pot inside the unit. Ensure the pot's indent lines up with the rear bump of the main unit.
4. Confirm all the accessories are in place.
5. Turn on the device using the power button.
6. Turn the dial to choose the KEEP WARM function.
7. The default temperatures will display.
8. Now, set your appropriate cooking duration according to your recipe. Using the arrow buttons, you can increase or decrease the time by intervals of one minute for up to 1 hour or intervals of 5 minutes for up to 6 hours.
9. Press START/STOP, and the unit starts the count.
10. Once the time elapses, you will hear a beep from the unit, and the unit displays END.

Sous Vide Function

1. Open the lid. Always ensure your hands are dry.
2. Plug in the Ninja Foodi PossibleCooker.
3. Place the cooking pot inside the unit. Ensure the pot's indent lines up with the rear bump of the main unit. Add 12 cups of water at room temperature.
4. Confirm all the accessories are in place.
5. Turn on the device using the power button.
6. Turn the dial to choose the STEAM function.
7. Utilize the +/- TEMP arrows to adjust your temperature settings in intervals of 5 degrees to between 120°F and 190°F.
8. Now, set your appropriate cooking duration according to your recipe. The default is always 3 hours. Using the arrow buttons, you can increase or decrease the time by intervals of 15 minutes for up to 12 hours or intervals of 1 hour for 12 to 24 hours.
9. Ready to preheat? Press the start/stop button. The screen will display 'PRE,' and a progress bar will show the progress. This process might take around 5 minutes, but it varies based on your chosen temperature.
10. Once preheated, you'll hear a beep, and the screen will prompt you with an "Add Food" display. It is time to add your ingredients.
11. Lift the lid and arrange your food inside the cooking pot. Shut the lid, and your cooking starts with the timer ticking away.
12. Once the cooking time elapses, you will hear a beep from the unit, and the unit displays END.

13. Once the cooking time elapses, you will hear a beep from the unit, and it will automatically transition to the KEEP WARM mode while counting up.

Braise Function

1. Open the lid. Always ensure your hands are dry.
2. Plug in the Ninja Foodi PossibleCooker.
3. Place the cooking pot inside the unit. Ensure the pot's indent lines up with the rear bump of the main unit.
4. Confirm all the accessories are in place.
5. Turn on the device using the power button.
6. You need to sear the ingredients first using the instructions for the sear/saute function.
7. Once the searing is complete, use stock or wine to deglaze. (Note: Add 1 cup of liquid to your pot for successful deglazing. Scrape the brown bits to the pot's bottom and mix with the cooking liquid.)
8. Pour the rest of the cooking liquid and your ingredients into your pot.
9. Turn the dial to choose the BRAISE function.
10. The default temperature will display.
11. Now, set your appropriate cooking duration according to your recipe. Use the +/- TIME arrows to set cook time in 15-minute increments.
12. Press the start/stop button to start the process.
13. Once the cooking time elapses, you will hear a beep from the unit, and the unit displays END for about 5 minutes.

Bake Function:

1. Ensure the lid is open. Your hands should always be dry.
2. Plug in the Ninja Foodi Possible Cooker.
3. Set the cooking pot inside the unit, ensuring the pot's indent matches the main unit's bump. Securely close the hood afterward.
4. Confirm all accessories are in place.
5. Turn the Ninja Foodi PossibleCooker on using the power button.
6. Now, select the BAKE function. A default temperature will be displayed. Adjust it using the up and down arrows as needed. It should be between 250°F and 425°F.

NOTE: Adapting a traditional oven recipe? Lower your baking temperature by 25°F. And remember, frequent checks prevent overcooking.

7. Decide on your baking duration next. With the up and down arrows, you can set the time, increasing in 1-minute intervals for as long as 1 hour or 5-minute intervals for up to 6 hours.

8. Initiate the preheating by pressing the start button. 'PRE' will be shown on the display, accompanied by a progress bar. This preheating phase might last around 3 minutes but varies based on your set temperature.
NOTE: Preheating is advised for optimum results. However, if you're crunched for time, a second press of the 9BAKE button bypasses it. The "Add Food" prompt will appear, signaling it's time to introduce your ingredients.

9. On completing the preheat, an alert will sound, and "Add Food" will be displayed.

10. Lift the hood and either place your ingredients in the pot or position your baking pan at the pot's base. Once the lid is shut, the baking starts, and the timer ticks.
NOTE: You can open the hood anytime for a quick check or a gentle stir. The timer will hold and continue once you close the lid again.

11. You'll hear a beep at the end of your set baking time, and 'END' will pop up on the screen for 5 minutes. For a faster cooldown, leave the lid up after taking out your baked goodies. Be cautious - the device's outer layer can be hot. If your baked treat needs more time, adjust with the up arrow and press start.

Proof Function:
1. Place dough in the pot and place the lid on top.
2. Turn the dial to select PROOF. The default temperature setting will display.
3. Use the +/- TEMP arrows to set temperature. in 5-degree increments between 90°F and 105°F.
4. Use the +/- TIME arrows to adjust the proof time in 5-minute increments.
5. Press START/STOP to begin cooking.
6. When cook time reaches zero, unit will beep, and END will flash 3 times on the display.
NOTE: If you poke perfectly proofed dough with your finger, the indentation will hold its shape and disappear slowly. If more proofing is needed, the dough will spring back and not hold the indentation.

Tips for Using Accessories
When you cook using the Ninja Foodi PossibleCooker, you will realize that there are a number of accessories that enhance your cooking. Let's check the tips on using these accessories.

Spoon-Ladle: It is a multifunctional tool that goes beyond serving. You can use it to taste, stir, and label delicious meals. Its unique design gives you ample time when using it in the pot.

Top Pot Handle/Spoon-Ladle Rest: Whenever you are not using the spoon-ladle, you can set it on the top pot handle for resting. This is good, especially in minimizing mess and organizing your space.

Cooking Lid: It is a preservative of your flavors. You add it on the top of the pot to seal in moisture during various cooking modes, ensuring flavor is infused in your dishes.

Side Pot Handles: These handles offer a secure grip when transferring the cooking pot.

8.5-Quart Cooking Pot: This is where all the magic happens. It is very spacious and allows for even distribution of heat. Preheat it before you add your ingredients. The nonstick surface allows for easy cleanup.

Main Unit: It acts as the brain of your cooking operation. Make sure you set it on a flat, stable surface, and there should be adequate ventilation to get optimal performance.

Control Panel: This is the command center. You can choose the cooking functions and adjust temperatures and time settings.

Straight from the Store

Once you buy a brand new Ninja Foodi PossibleCooker, you will find the following in the box:

The 8.5-quart Cooking Pot
• Base Unit
• Detachable Spoon-Ladle
• Glass Cooking Lid
• Recipe Guide.

Choosing Your Ingredients:

Here are the tips on selecting the appropriate ingredients.

1. Go for fresh produce. It could be succulent fruits or crisp vegetables (check for firm textures, fragrant aroma, and vibrant colors).
2. Choose the best fresh cuts of meats with a good balance of fat to enhance the flavor and tenderness. Go for bright, red coloration.
3. Select fresh, aromatic spices and store them well in a cool, dark place. Avoid the expired ones.
4. Go for fresh dairy delights (milk, cheese, or yogurt).
5. Do not stock expired grains or canned goods.
6. Select fresh seafood with firm flesh.
7. Always check with the seasons to ensure you take advantage of the seasonal produce. You can get fresh and affordable seasonal fruits and veggies.

Cleaning and Caring for Ninja Foodi PossibleCooker

Cleaning of the unit should happen after every use. Before cleaning, ensure the unit is turned off, unplugged, and completely cooled down. Once your meal is out, leave the pot open for faster cooling.

A simple wipe with a damp cloth does the trick when it comes to the main unit or cooker base and the control panel. No fuss, no mess.

Hand wash the cooking pot. If any residues are stuck in the pot, fill it with water and give it time to soak.

For the other accessories, easily clean them by popping them in the dishwasher.

Air dry them before storage.

A golden rule to remember? Keep those harsh scrubbers and cleaning agents away. And, for goodness sake, don't submerge the main unit in water.

Frequently Asked Questions & Notes

Do I need to preheat it?
Yes, just like an oven. Preheating ensures even cooking.

Can I use metal utensils on it?
Best not to. Stick with wooden or silicone to prevent scratches.
Why won't my PossibleCooker turn on?
Check the plug and power source. Reset your circuit breaker if necessary.

The timer's not working. What do I do?
Reset the unit. If issues persist, reach out to customer service.

How often should I clean it?
Clean all removable parts after every use. Wipe the base unit when needed.

When do I add Ingredients?
After the preheat finishes.

There's a weird smell when I use it. Normal?
New appliances often have a scent. It should fade after a few uses.

Can I use the appliance for baking?
Yes. Make sure you use the right settings.

Why did the unit turn off?
If no function is selected within 10 minutes of turning it on, it shuts down automatically.

Why is the unit counting up instead of counting down?
The unit is in Keep Warm mode after completing the Slow Cook cycle.

Handy Notes:
Safety First: Always use oven mitts when handling hot parts.
Ventilation: Ensure your kitchen is well-ventilated to reduce smoke and odors.
Experiment: Get creative and test new recipes or your own composition.
Storage: Store in a cool, dry place. Do not add heavy items on top.
Children: Always keep out of reach of children when not in use.

4-Week Diet Plan

Week 1

Day 1:
Breakfast: Orange-Almond Oats Muffins
Lunch: Spicy Garlic Beans
Snack: Gingered Teriyaki Mushrooms
Dinner: Spicy Beef and Brown Rice Casserole
Dessert: Cherry-Oats Cobbler

Day 2:
Breakfast: Eggy Waffle and Bacon Casserole
Lunch: Cashew and Carrot Rice Pilaf
Snack: Spicy Lime Corn
Dinner: Creamy Chicken Divan and Broccoli
Dessert: Caramel Apple Oats Crumble

Day 3:
Breakfast: Italian Sausage Cornbread Strata
Lunch: Quinoa & Mushroom–Stuffed Peppers
Snack: Asian Turkey Meatballs
Dinner: Beef Brisket Stew with Pearl Barley and Celery
Dessert: Delicious Peanut Butter Fondue

Day 4:
Breakfast: Chicken & Ham Strata with Currant Jelly Sauce
Lunch: Garlicky Sweet Potatoes & Parsley
Snack: Garlicky Mashed Potatoes
Dinner: Slow-Cooker BBQ Pork
Dessert: Nutty Cherry Bread Pudding

Day 5:
Breakfast: Chocolate Banana Overnight Oatmeal
Lunch: Cheesy Ziti and Zucchini
Snack: Hummus and Pickles Salad
Dinner: Herbed Chicken with Beans and Bacon
Dessert: Chocolate Cheesecake

Day 6:
Breakfast: Breakfast Grits
Lunch: Caribbean Black Beans, Tomato and Rice
Snack: Sweet & Sour Butternut Squash and Brussels Sprouts
Dinner: Quinoa, Beans and Turkey Chili
Dessert: Easy Blueberry Muffins

Day 7:
Breakfast: Potato Cheese Frittata
Lunch: Spicy Eggplant Cubes
Snack: Maple-Orange Kale
Dinner: Lamb and Parsnips Stew
Dessert: Apricots Pancakes

Week 2

Day 1:
Breakfast: Cheesy Ham and Corn Casserole
Lunch: Coconut Sweet Potatoes Hash
Snack: Parmesan-Garlic Green Beans
Dinner: Apricot and Cube Steaks Stew
Dessert: Savory Crème Brûlée

Day 2:
Breakfast: Pear and French Toast Casserole with Pecans
Lunch: Sweet and Spicy Peanut Pasta with Celery
Snack: Maple-Orange Glazed Carrots
Dinner: Quinoa, Beans and Turkey Chili
Dessert: Lime Pots de Crème

Day 3:
Breakfast: Italian Sausage Cornbread Strata
Lunch: Creamy Baby Peas and Rice Casserol
Snack: Honey and Vinegar Glazed Cabbage and Apples
Dinner: Chicken and Chickpea Stew
Dessert: Vanilla Apricot Rice Pudding

Day 4:
Breakfast: Breakfast Apple Risotto
Lunch: Cheesy Red Potato & Bell Pepper Casserole
Snack: Simple Baked Chickpeas with Herbs
Dinner: Pork, Beans and Meatballs
Dessert: Toffee Peach Crumble

Day 5:
Breakfast: Honey-Lime Quinoa and Berries Salad
Lunch: Cheesy Farro and Pea Risotto
Snack: Buffalo Chicken Wings
Dinner: Lime Steak Fajitas
Dessert: Classic Apple Pie Filling

Day 6:
Breakfast: Sausage and Potato Egg Casserole
Lunch: Lemon Chickpeas and Wheat Pilaf
Snack: Cheesy Chicken Enchilada Dip
Dinner: Lemongrass Turkey & Pak Choy Soup
Dessert: Fruity Wine–Poached Pears

Day 7:
Breakfast: Potato Cheese Frittata
Lunch: Cheesy Carrot
Snack: Sweet-and-Spicy Meatballs with Pineapple
Dinner: Cheese Lamb Burritos
Dessert: Mixed Berries Cobbler

Day 1:
Breakfast: Sausage and Potato Egg Casserole
Lunch: Lemon-Cheese Risotto
Snack: Classic Hummus
Dinner: Beef and Beans in Barbecue Sauce
Dessert: Sweet Pumpkin Butter

Day 2:
Breakfast: Honey-Lime Quinoa and Berries Salad
Lunch: Spicy Bean & Rice–Stuffed Bell Peppers
Snack: Rosemary Bakes Potatoes and Beets
Dinner: Thyme Chicken Pot Pie
Dessert: Chocolate Chia Seeds Pudding with Berries

Day 3:
Breakfast: Chorizo, Brussels Sprouts and Sweet Potato Hash
Lunch: Basil Chickpeas and Olives
Snack: Delicious Chicken Lettuce Wraps
Dinner: Pork and Potato Stew
Dessert: Chickpea Brownies

Day 4:
Breakfast: Avocado Toast with Basil-Walnuts Pesto
Lunch: Maple-Glazed Sweet Potatoes & Pecans
Snack: Chipotle Mayo Glazed Corn
Dinner: Creamy Mustard Pork Loin Chops
Dessert: Vanilla -Chocolate Fondue

Day 5:
Breakfast: Breakfast Apple Risotto
Lunch: Caramelized Onion Rings
Snack: Garlic Spaghetti Squash with Cheese
Dinner: Sweet & Sour Beef Short Ribs
Dessert: Maple Banana-Orange Sundaes

Day 6:
Breakfast: Orange-Almond Oats Muffins
Lunch: Cashew and Carrot Rice Pilaf
Snack: Asian Turkey Meatballs
Dinner: Honey-Teriyaki Chicken Thighs
Dessert: Mango Wontons

Day 7:
Breakfast: Italian Sausage Cornbread Strata
Lunch: Orange-Glazed Carrots with Raisins
Snack: Easy Slow-Cooked Sweet Potatoes
Dinner: Lamb & Rice Stew
Dessert: Delicious Chocolate-Mint Truffles

Day 1:
Breakfast: Sweet Potato, Quinoa and Black Bean Casserole
Lunch: Spicy Garlic Beans
Snack: Rice Cereal and Peanuts Party Mix
Dinner: Cheesy Steak and Pasta Soup
Dessert: Dried Fruits and Rice Pudding

Day 2:
Breakfast: Chocolate Banana Overnight Oatmeal
Lunch: Garlicky Sweet Potatoes & Parsley
Snack: Hot Chicken Wings with Blue Cheese Dip
Dinner: Creamy Chicken Tikka Masala
Dessert: Maple Hot Chocolate

Day 3:
Breakfast: Chicken & Ham Strata with Currant Jelly Sauce
Lunch: Wild Rice and Grape Tomato Salad
Snack: Cheese Spinach-Artichoke Dip
Dinner: Delicious Beef Barley Soup
Dessert: Caramel Apple Oats Crumble

Day 4:
Breakfast: Breakfast Grits
Lunch: Quinoa & Mushroom–Stuffed Peppers
Snack: Pineapple Turkey Meatballs
Dinner: Spiced Pork Roast
Dessert: Cherry-Oats Cobbler

Day 5:
Breakfast: Potato Cheese Frittata
Lunch: Spicy Eggplant Cubes
Snack: Creamy Garlic Cauliflower
Dinner: Creamy Mustard Pork Loin Chops
Dessert: Easy Blueberry Muffins

Day 6:
Breakfast: Breakfast Apple Risotto
Lunch: Coconut Sweet Potatoes Hash
Snack: Gingered Teriyaki Mushrooms
Dinner: Lemony Whole Turkey with Vegetables
Dessert: Chocolate Cheesecake

Day 7:
Breakfast: Cheesy Egg and Broccoli Breakfast Casserole
Lunch: Mayo Chicken and Grapes Salad
Snack: Garlicky Mashed Potatoes
Dinner: Ham, Peas and Cheese Potatoes
Dessert: Fruity Wine–Poached Pear

Eggy Waffle and Bacon Casserole

Prep Time: 15 minutes | Cook Time: 6 hours | Serves: 8

Unsalted butter, for greasing
10 large eggs
1 cup milk
¾ cup apple juice
¼ teaspoon ground nutmeg

1 (30-ounce) box whole grain frozen waffles, cut into 2-inch pieces
1 cup dried cherries
8 slices precooked bacon, chopped
1½ cups (12 ounces) creamy goat cheese, cubed

1. Grease the inside of the pot thoroughly with butter. 2. Add the eggs, milk, apple juice, and nutmeg to the pot and beat until thoroughly mixed. 3. Stir in the waffle pieces, cherries, bacon, and cheese. 4. Cover and turn the dial to Slow Cook, cook on Low for about 6 hours, or until the casserole is set and puffed. Spoon out of the pot to serve. 5. Store leftovers covered in the refrigerator for up to 4 days. Do not freeze.

Per Serving: Calories 299; Fat 23.24g; Sodium 345mg; Carbs 10.14g; Fiber 0.5g; Sugar 7.33g; Protein 12.43g

Italian Sausage Cornbread Strata

Prep Time: 15 minutes | Cook Time: 3-3½ hours | Serves: 5

½ pound hot bulk Italian sausage
1 onion, chopped
1 cup flour
½ cup yellow cornmeal
2 tablespoons sugar
1 teaspoon baking powder

½ teaspoon baking soda
½ teaspoon salt
2 eggs
½ cup whole milk
¼ cup butter, melted
½ cup shredded Colby cheese

1. Add sausage and onions to the pot, stir to combine. Turn dial to Sear/Sauté, set temperature to HI, and press START/STOP to begin cooking. Stirring to break up sausage, until sausage is cooked. Drain well and transfer to a bowl. 2. Mix together flour, sugar, cornmeal, baking soda, baking powder, and salt in a big bowl. In a separate medium-sized bowl, combine eggs, milk, and butter, and mix thoroughly. Then add the egg mixture to the dry ingredients, and stir until just combined. 3. Spray the inside of the pot with nonstick baking spray containing flour. Place half of the batter in the pot; top with half of the sausage and half of the cheese. Repeat layers. 4. Cover with the lid. Turn dial to Slow Cook, set temperature to HI, and set time to 3 - 3½ hours. Press START/STOP to begin cooking, cook until cornbread tests done when tested with a toothpick. 5. Serve immediately by spooning out of the pot as in spoon bread.

Per Serving: Calories 495; Fat 26.84g; Sodium 969mg; Carbs 45.63g; Fiber 3g; Sugar 7.85g; Protein 19.89g

Orange–Almond Oats Muffins

Prep Time: 15 minutes | Cook Time: 22 minutes | Serves: 6

1 large egg, separated
1 teaspoon extra-virgin olive oil
2 tablespoons nonfat Greek yogurt
2 teaspoons almond extract
1½ cups gluten-free oat flour
2 tablespoons wheat germ
1 teaspoon baking powder

½ teaspoon baking soda
1 teaspoon orange zest
½ cup slivered blanched almonds, divided
¼ cup low-fat buttermilk
⅓ cup orange juice
2 teaspoons light brown sugar

1. In a medium bowl, beat the egg yolk with a whisk until frothy. Add the olive oil and whisk some more. Add the Greek yogurt and almond extract while whisking. 2. In another medium bowl, mix together the oat flour, wheat germ, baking powder, baking soda, orange zest, and ¼ cup of the almonds. 3. Gently fold the egg yolk mixture into the flour mixture. 4. In another medium bowl, whisk the egg whites until frothy and white. Fold it into the muffin batter. 5. Slowly add the buttermilk and orange juice, gently mixing after each addition until smooth. 6. Place the batter in the pot. Sprinkle the top with the brown sugar and the remaining ¼ cup almonds. 7. Cover and turn the dial to Bake. Bake at 375°F for 20 to 22 minutes or until a toothpick inserted in the center comes out clean.

Per Serving: Calories 163; Fat 5.15g; Sodium 164mg; Carbs 22.33g; Fiber 2.1g; Sugar 3.14g; Protein 7.09g

Cheesy Ham and Corn Casserole

Prep Time: 15 minutes | Cook Time: 3-4 hours | Serves: 6

1 onion, chopped
1 tablespoon olive oil
5 eggs
¾ cup milk
2 tablespoons flour
1 cup shredded Swiss cheese

1 tablespoon sugar
⅛ teaspoon pepper
1 (10-ounce) package frozen corn, thawed
1 cup chopped smoked ham
¼ cup grated Parmesan cheese

1. Add olive oil and onion to the pot. Turn dial to Sear/Sauté, set temperature to HI, and press START/STOP to begin cooking. Sauté the onion in olive oil until crisp-tender. Remove from the pot and cool for 10 minutes. 2. Whisk the eggs in a big bowl until they become frothy and well-combined. Then, add the milk and whisk thoroughly. Add the flour, Swiss cheese, sugar, pepper, corn, and ham to the mixture and stir until everything is evenly mixed. Finally, add the cooled sautéed onions and stir them in. 3. Pour into the pot and top with Parmesan cheese. Cover with the lid and turn dial to Slow Cook, set temperature to HI, cook for 3–4 hours or until casserole is set. Serve immediately.

Per Serving: Calories 306; Fat 18.98g; Sodium 233mg; Carbs 16.65g; Fiber 1.4g; Sugar 7.64g; Protein 17.91g

Sausage and Potato Egg Casserole

Prep Time: 15 minutes | Cook Time: 6-8 hours | Serves: 12

1 tablespoon butter

6 cups frozen hash browns, thawed

1 pound cooked, crumbled breakfast sausage

12 eggs

1 cup half-and-half

3 cups shredded cheddar cheese

1 teaspoon sea salt

1. Coat the inside of the pot with the butter, making sure to cover about two-thirds up the sides of the pot. 2. Layer half of the hash browns and half of the sausage in the pot. Repeat with the remaining hash browns and sausage. 3. Whisk together the eggs, cheese, half-and-half, and salt in a bowl. Pour the mixture into the pot. 4. Cover and turn the dial to Slow Cook, cook on low for 6 to 8 hours, or until the casserole is fully set. Let it cool for at least 10 minutes before serving.

Per Serving: Calories 577; Fat 41.56g; Sodium 552mg; Carbs 25.04g; Fiber 2.4g; Sugar 1.9g; Protein 26.89g

Chicken & Ham Strata with Currant Jelly Sauce

Prep Time: 15 minutes | Cook Time: 3 hours | Serves: 6

8 slices sourdough bread, cubed

1 (12-ounce) can chicken, drained

1 cup shredded Swiss cheese

½ cup chopped cooked ham

6 eggs

½ cup heavy cream

½ teaspoon salt

⅛ teaspoon pepper

½ teaspoon dried oregano leaves

3 tablespoons cider vinegar

¼ cup currant jelly

3 tablespoons water

2 tablespoons honey

½ teaspoon paprika

2 tablespoons butter

¼ cup powdered sugar

½ cup crisp rice cereal crumbs

1. Spray the inside of the pot with nonstick cooking spray. Layer cubed bread, chicken, cheese, and ham in it. 2. In a big bowl, combine eggs, cream, pepper, salt, and oregano; beat well. Pour into the pot. Let mixture stand for 20 minutes, pushing bread back down into the egg mixture as necessary. Cover with the lid and turn the dial to Slow Cook. Cook on HI for 3 hours or until egg mixture is set. 3. Mix vinegar, jelly, water, honey, paprika, and butter in a small saucepan. Heat until it simmers, then lower the heat and continue to simmer for 8-9 minutes while stirring frequently, until the sauce is well combined and slightly thickened. 4. To serve the strata, remove it from the pot and pour the currant jelly sauce over it. Sprinkle with powdered sugar and cereal crumbs, and serve right away.

Per Serving: Calories 913; Fat 32.69g; Sodium 1635mg; Carbs 110.68g; Fiber 4.4g; Sugar 20.09g; Protein 44.14g

Sweet Potato, Quinoa and Black Bean Casserole

Prep Time: 15 minutes | Cook Time: 6-8 hours | Serves: 6

1 tablespoon canola oil, or nonstick cooking spray
2 cups quinoa, rinsed
4 cups vegetable broth, or store-bought
2 medium sweet potatoes, peeled and diced
1 cup canned black beans, drained and rinsed
1 cup frozen corn kernels, thawed

1 teaspoon ground cumin
1 teaspoon smoked paprika
1 teaspoon sea salt
¼ cup minced fresh cilantro
1 lime, halved

1. Coat the inside of the pot with the oil or spray it with nonstick cooking spray. 2. Add the quinoa, vegetable broth, black beans, corn, sweet potatoes, paprika, cumin, and sea salt to the pot. Stir gently to mix. 3. Cover and turn the dial to Slow Cook, cook on low heat for 6 to 8 hours, or until the quinoa is tender. 4. Stir in the cilantro and squeeze the lime halves over the top. Serve.

Per Serving: Calories 400; Fat 7.83g; Sodium 784mg; Carbs 68.89g; Fiber 10.4g; Sugar 6.18g; Protein 15.08g

Potato Cheese Frittata

Prep Time: 15 minutes | Cook Time: 4-5 hours | Serves: 5

1 (16-ounce) package frozen hash brown potatoes
1 onion, diced
2 cloves garlic, minced
¾ cup shredded Cheddar cheese
¼ cup shredded Muenster cheese
6 eggs

½ cup sour cream
½ teaspoon salt
⅛ teaspoon pepper
1 cup chopped canned apricots
2 tablespoons honey
2 teaspoons fresh thyme leaves

1. Spray a pot with nonstick cooking spray. Layer potatoes, onions, garlic, and cheeses in it. 2. In a big bowl, combine eggs and sour cream and blend well. Stir in salt and pepper and mix well. Pour into the pot. 3. Cover with the lid and turn the dial to Slow Cook, cook on high for 4–5 hours or until eggs are set. Mix together the apricots, honey, and thyme in a medium bowl. Serve apricot topping with frittata.

Per Serving: Calories 453; Fat 21.96g; Sodium 828mg; Carbs 45.31g; Fiber 4.2g; Sugar 22.96g; Protein 20.3g

Pear and French Toast Casserole with Pecans

Prep Time: 15 minutes | Cook Time: 6 hours | Serves: 8

Unsalted butter, for greasing
9 large eggs
2 cups milk
½ cup brown sugar
2 teaspoons vanilla extract
¼ teaspoon ground nutmeg

11 slices whole grain bread
1 cup mascarpone cheese
3 Bosc pears, cored and chopped
2 cups whole small pecans
1 cup golden raisins

1. Grease the pot thoroughly with butter. 2. Add the eggs, milk, vanilla, brown sugar, and nutmeg to the pot and beat until thoroughly mixed. 3. Coat the bread slices evenly with the mascarpone cheese and cut into 2-inch cubes. 4. Add the coated bread cubes, pears, pecans, and raisins to the egg mixture in the pot and stir gently. 5. Cover and turn the dial to Slow Cook, cook on Low for about 6 hours, or until the casserole registers 160°F on a food thermometer and the mixture is puffed and set. Spoon out of the pot to serve. 6. Store leftovers covered in the refrigerator for up to 4 days. Do not freeze.
Per Serving: Calories 622; Fat 32.97g; Sodium 356mg; Carbs 66.51g; Fiber 9g; Sugar 36.76g; Protein 19.75g

Honey-Lime Quinoa and Berries Salad

Prep Time: 10 minutes | Cook Time: 0 minutes | Serves: 4

For the Fruit Salad:
1 cup uncooked quinoa
1 cup sliced blackberries
1 cup sliced strawberries
1 cup sliced blueberries
For the Glaze:
¼ cup honey
2 tablespoons freshly squeezed lime juice

1 mango, diced
1 kiwi, sliced
1 tablespoon chopped fresh mint, for garnish

1 tablespoon chia seeds (optional)
2 to 3 tablespoons water

To make the fruit salad: 1. Rinse and prepare the quinoa according to package directions. Cool the quinoa to room temperature. 2. Combine the quinoa, blackberries, strawberries, blueberries, mango, and kiwi in a large bowl.
To make the glaze: 1. Mix together the honey, lime juice, chia seeds (if using), and water in a small bowl. 2. Drizzle the glaze over the fruit salad and toss to coat. Garnish with the fresh mint. Store the fruit salad in an airtight container in the refrigerator for 1 to 2 days.
Per Serving: Calories 541; Fat 10.04g; Sodium 603mg; Carbs 90.44g; Fiber 8.3g; Sugar 57.29g; Protein 27.13g

Breakfast Grits

Prep Time: 15 minutes | Cook Time: 7-8 hours | Serves: 4

Cooking spray or neutral-flavored oil, such as canola
1½ cups stone-ground grits
6 cups water

2 teaspoons salt
4 to 6 tablespoons vegan butter
Freshly ground black pepper

1. Grease the inside of the pot with cooking spray or oil. 2. Add the grits, water, and salt and mix well. 3. Cover with the lid and turn the dial to Slow Cook, cook on low for 7 to 8 hours. 4. Remove the lid. Scatter the vegan butter on top. Use a whisk to stir the grits until they reach an even consistency and the vegan butter has melted. 5. Season with pepper and serve.

Per Serving: Calories 253; Fat 18.82g; Sodium 1786mg; Carbs 20.27g; Fiber 1.3g; Sugar 0.59g; Protein 2.45g

Chocolate Banana Overnight Oatmeal

Prep Time: 8 hours | Cook Time: 0 minutes| Serves: 1

½ cup gluten-free rolled oats
½ tablespoon cocoa powder
1 teaspoon milk chocolate morsels
⅛ teaspoon cinnamon
¼ teaspoon pure vanilla extract

½ cup unsweetened coconut milk, plus more as needed
½ banana peeled and chopped
1 to 2 teaspoons pure maple syrup

1. Mix rolled oats, cocoa powder, chocolate chips, and cinnamon in a small mason jar. 2. Add vanilla extract, coconut milk, banana, and maple syrup, and stir well. 3. Cover and refrigerate for 8 hours or overnight. 4. Before serving, stir the mixture and add a little more coconut milk if necessary to reach your desired consistency.

Per Serving: Calories 475; Fat 32.52g; Sodium 25mg; Carbs 58.28g; Fiber 12.4g; Sugar 16.61g; Protein 12.19g

Breakfast Apple Risotto

Prep Time: 15 minutes | Cook Time: 6 hours | Serves: 4

4 cups nondairy milk
1½ cups Arborio rice
1 cup finely diced tart apples such as Granny Smith
⅓ cup packed brown sugar
2 tablespoons vegan butter, melted

2 teaspoons ground cinnamon
½ teaspoon salt
¼ teaspoon ground nutmeg
Optional garnish: dried fruit

1. Add the nondairy milk, Arborio rice, apples, vegan butter, brown sugar, cinnamon, salt, and nutmeg to the pot; mix thoroughly. 2. Cover and turn the dial to Slow Cook, cook on low for 6 hours or on high for 4 to 5 hours. 3. Garnish with dried fruit (if using), and serve.

Per Serving: Calories 428; Fat 23.09g; Sodium 449mg; Carbs 56.29g; Fiber 10.8g; Sugar 32.98g; Protein 13.86g

Chorizo, Brussels Sprouts and Sweet Potato Hash

Prep Time: 15 minutes | Cook Time: 45 minutes | Serves: 8

For the Sausage:

1 tablespoon ground cumin

1 tablespoon sodium-free garlic powder

1 tablespoon sodium-free onion powder

1 tablespoon pimentón (Spanish paprika)

1 teaspoon freshly ground black pepper

1 teaspoon sodium-free chili pepper

1 teaspoon ground cloves

1 teaspoon ground coriander

1 teaspoon dried thyme

½ teaspoon cayenne pepper

1-pound low-sodium ground pork

2 tablespoons cider vinegar

Zest of 1 lime

For the Hash:

1 (1-pound) container fresh baby or mature Brussels sprouts (or 1 package frozen)

2 Granny Smith apples, cored and cubed

2 large sweet potatoes, peeled and cubed

1 medium zucchini, peeled, seeded, and cubed.

1 medium yellow onion, diced

2 tablespoons extra-virgin olive oil

For the Glaze:

¼ cup pure maple syrup

2 tablespoons extra-virgin olive oil

2 tablespoons balsamic vinegar

1 tablespoon chipotle pepper

Freshly ground black pepper

To make the sausage: 1. In a mortar and pestle or a grinder, grind together the cumin, garlic powder, black pepper, onion powder, pimentón, chili pepper, coriander, cloves, thyme, and cayenne. 2. Add the ground spices, pork, vinegar, and lime zest to a large bowl and mix well. 3. Let the sausage sit in the refrigerator for 10 to 20 minutes before cooking to let the spices meld. If desired, divide it into 8 small balls and form patties.

To make the hash: 1. In the meantime, prepare the hash. Generously grease the pot with olive oil. 2. If using mature Brussels sprouts, remove any tough outer leaves cut them in half. Leave frozen or baby Brussels sprouts whole. Transfer to a large bowl. 3. Add the apples, sweet potatoes, zucchini, and onions, and drizzle with olive oil.

To make the glaze: 1. Mix together the maple syrup, olive oil, vinegar, chipotle pepper, and season with black pepper. 2. Toss the glaze with the vegetables and spread them out in one layer in the pot. Turn the dial to Bake and set the temperature to 400°F. Bake until sweet potatoes are tender and Brussels sprouts are lightly browned, 25 to 30 minutes. 3. Mix in the chorizo and return to the pot to bake another 10 to 15 minutes. Once the vegetables are cooked through, toss and serve.

Per Serving: Calories 263; Fat 8.06g; Sodium 647mg; Carbs 32.85g; Fiber 6g; Sugar 15.92g; Protein 16.48g

Avocado Toast with Basil–Walnuts Pesto

Prep Time: 15 minutes | Cook Time: 5 minutes | Serves: 2

For the Pesto:
⅓ cup fresh basil leaves, loosely packed
¼ cup walnuts
Juice of 1 lemon
⅛ teaspoon freshly ground black pepper

⅛ teaspoon garlic powder
1 tablespoon extra-virgin olive oil
1 tablespoon hot water

For the Toast:
3 slices crusty whole-grain bread
1 avocado, sliced
Microgreens, for garnish

Freshly ground black pepper
Extra-virgin olive oil (optional)
Lemon wedges (optional)

To make the pesto: 1. Combine the basil, walnuts, black pepper, lemon juice, garlic powder, olive oil, and water in a blender or food processor. 2. Blend until smooth, with some nut pieces remaining for texture.

To make the toast: 1. Toast the bread. 2. Divide the avocado slices equally among the toast slices. 3. Spread 2 tablespoons of the pesto over the avocado. Add the microgreens to garnish and season with black pepper. 4. Drizzle with additional olive oil and lemon juice (if using), and serve immediately.

Per Serving: Calories 423; Fat 26.92g; Sodium 302mg; Carbs 38.5g; Fiber 12.1g; Sugar 5.47g; Protein 11.91g

Cheesy Egg and Broccoli Breakfast Casserole

Prep Time: 15 minutes | Cook Time: 6-8 hours | Serves: 6-8

1 tablespoon butter
6 cups frozen hash browns, thawed
4 cups diced broccoli
1 red bell pepper, diced

12 eggs
1 cup half-and-half
2 cups shredded pepper jack cheese
1½ teaspoons sea salt

1. Coat the inside of the pot with the butter, making sure to cover about two-thirds up the sides of the pot. 2. Layer half of the hash browns, half of the broccoli, and half of the bell pepper in the pot. Repeat with the remaining hash browns, broccoli, and bell pepper. 3. In a bowl, whisk together the eggs, half-and-half, cheese, and salt. Pour the mixture to the pot. 4. Cover and turn the dial to Slow Cook, cook on low for 6 to 8 hours, or until the casserole is fully set. Let it cool for at least 10 minutes before serving.

Per Serving: Calories 669; Fat 43.75g; Sodium 941mg; Carbs 43.12g; Fiber 4.8g; Sugar 3.71g; Protein 28.29g

Chapter 2 Vegetables and Sides

Cashew and Carrot Rice Pilaf

Prep Time: 15 minutes | Cook Time: 6-7 hours | Serves: 6

1 tablespoon olive oil
1 onion, chopped
2 cloves garlic, minced
½ cup wild rice
1 cup long grain brown rice
2½ cups water

½ teaspoon salt
⅛ teaspoon pepper
½ teaspoon dried thyme leaves
2 carrots, sliced
½ cup chopped toasted cashews
3 tablespoons chopped flat-leaf parsley

1. Add olive oil to the pot and turn the dial to Sear/Sauté, set temperature to LO, and press START/STOP to begin cooking. 2. Once the oil is heated, add onion and garlic; cook and stir for 4 minutes until crisp-tender. Add wild and brown rice; cook for 1 minute. Add water, salt, and pepper; bring to a boil Press START/STOP to turn off the Sear/Sauté function. 3. Add thyme and carrots. Cover and turn the dial to Slow Cook, cook on low heat for 6–7 hours or until rice is tender. Stir in cashews and parsley and serve immediately.

Per Serving: Calories 323; Fat 14.67g; Sodium 267mg; Carbs 42.76g; Fiber 3.1g; Sugar 3.45g; Protein 7.48g

Spicy Garlic Beans

Prep Time: 15 minutes | Cook Time: 10 hours | Serves: 12

4 cups savory vegetable broth or low-sodium vegetable broth
4 cups water
3 cups dried pinto beans
1 onion, chopped
2 jalapeño peppers, minced

4 garlic cloves, minced
1 tablespoon chili powder
2 teaspoons ground cumin
1 teaspoon sweet paprika
1 teaspoon salt
½ teaspoon freshly ground black pepper

1. Combine all of the ingredients in the pot. Cover and turn the dial to Slow Cook, cook on high for 10 hours. 2. If there is quite a bit of liquid remaining after cooking, use a ladle to remove some, reserving it in a bowl. Using an immersion blender, blend until smooth or to your desired consistency, adding back the reserved liquid as needed. 3. Serve hot, or freeze in 1- or 2-cup portions in airtight containers.

Per Serving: Calories 196; Fat 1.09g; Sodium 269mg; Carbs 35.97g; Fiber 8.6g; Sugar 4.25g; Protein 11.61g

Quinoa & Mushroom–Stuffed Peppers

Prep Time: 15 minutes | Cook Time: 7-8 hours | Serves: 6

6 large green, red, orange, or yellow bell peppers, or a combination
2 (15-ounce) cans black beans, drained and rinsed
1 cup quinoa, rinsed
1 cup chopped onion
1 cup chopped button mushrooms
½ cup chopped red bell pepper
1 cup spicy salsa

1 tablespoon chopped fresh cilantro
1 teaspoon ground cumin
1 cup creamy queso dip or 1 cup shredded low-fat cheese, divided
Nonstick cooking spray
½ cup water
Freshly ground black pepper

1. Cut the tops off the peppers using a small knife and remove the stem and seeds. Reach inside and pull out any white bits of membrane that may remain. If any peppers do not stand up on their own, slice a very small amount off the bottom to create a flat bottom. 2. Combine together the beans, quinoa, onion, mushrooms, chopped bell pepper, salsa, cilantro, cumin, and ½ cup of queso in a large bowl. Fill each pepper with the quinoa mixture. 3. Spray the inside of the pot with cooking spray. Pour ½ cup of water into the bottom of the pot. Place the peppers in the pot so they are sitting in the water. Cover and turn the dial to Slow Cook, cook on low for 7 to 8 hours. 4. In the last 30 minutes of cooking, remove the lid and pour the remaining ½ cup of queso sauce over the peppers and cover again until everything is heated through. 5. Serve hot.

Per Serving: Calories 263; Fat 7.55g; Sodium 507mg; Carbs 37.56g; Fiber 7.2g; Sugar 11.19g; Protein 14.98g

Garlicky Sweet Potatoes & Parsley

Prep Time: 15 minutes | Cook Time: 6 hours | Serves: 8

½ cup margarine
6 cloves garlic, minced
1 onion, diced
1½ pounds red potatoes, quartered
½ cup unsweetened soymilk or rice milk

1 teaspoon salt
¼ teaspoon black pepper
¼ cup packed parsley leaves, chopped
1 tablespoon fresh lemon juice

1. Add the margarine to the pot. Turn dial to Sear/Sauté, set temperature to HI, and press START/STOP to begin cooking. 2. Add the garlic and onion, cook until they are golden brown, about 2–3 minutes. Press START/STOP to turn off the Sear/Sauté function. 3. Add the rest of the ingredients except for the parsley and lemon juice. Cover and turn the dial to Slow Cook, cook on low for 6 hours. 4. Mix in the parsley and lemon and serve.

Per Serving: Calories 175; Fat 11.66g; Sodium 319mg; Carbs 16.5g; Fiber 1.9g; Sugar 2.16g; Protein 2.37g

Cheesy Ziti and Zucchini

Prep Time: 15 minutes | Cook Time: 6 hours | Serves: 6

2½ cups marinara sauce
2½ cups low-sodium vegetable broth
½ pound mushrooms, sliced
½ pound zucchini, sliced
1 onion, chopped
2 garlic cloves, minced

½ teaspoon salt
1 teaspoon dried basil
1 teaspoon dried parsley
1-pound uncooked ziti
1 cup shredded low-fat mozzarella cheese

1. Add the tomatoes, marinara sauce, mushrooms, zucchini, broth, onion, basil, garlic, salt, and parsley to the pot. Stir to mix well. 2. Cover and turn the dial to Slow Cook, cook on low for about 6 hours. 3. Stir in the uncooked pasta, and top with the mozzarella cheese. Cook for 15 to 30 minutes more, or until the pasta is tender and the cheese is melted, and serve.
Per Serving: Calories 455; Fat 7.62g; Sodium 471mg; Carbs 91.97g; Fiber 13.1g; Sugar 51.01g; Protein 16.18g

Spicy Eggplant Cubes

Prep Time: 15 minutes | Cook Time: 6 hours | Serves: 6

Cooking spray
6 Japanese eggplants, rinsed and cubed
2 tablespoons balsamic vinegar
1 tablespoon hoisin sauce
1 tablespoon vegetable oil

1 teaspoon chili paste, such as sambal oelek
2 cloves garlic, minced
1 tablespoon sesame seeds
2 scallions, green parts only, chopped

1. Lightly spray the inside of the pot with the cooking spray. Add the cubed eggplant. 2. In a medium bowl, combine the remaining ingredients except the sesame seeds and scallions and pour over the eggplant cubes. 3. Cover and turn the dial to Slow Cook, cook on low for about 6 hours or until eggplant is very tender. 4. Transfer eggplant to a serving dish. Sprinkle on the sesame seeds and chopped scallion before serving.
Per Serving: Calories 185; Fat 4.34g; Sodium 73mg; Carbs 36.38g; Fiber 17.3g; Sugar 21.84g; Protein 6.11g

Caribbean Black Beans, Tomato and Rice

Prep Time: 15 minutes | Cook Time: 7-8 hours | Serves: 4

2 tablespoons olive oil
2 onions, chopped
3 cloves garlic, minced
1 green bell pepper
1 cup long grain brown rice
1 (15-ounce) can black beans
1 tomato, chopped

2 cups water
1 tablespoon vinegar
½ teaspoon Tabasco
½ teaspoon salt
¼ teaspoon pepper
3 tablespoons chopped cilantro

1. Add olive oil to the pot and turn the dial to Sear/Sauté, set temperature to LO, and press START/STOP to begin cooking. Once the oil is heated, add onion and garlic; cook and stir for 4 minutes. Press the START/STOP button to turn off the Sear/Sauté function. 2. Add the remaining ingredients except cilantro. Cover and turn the dial to Slow Cook, cook on low heat for 7–8 hours or until rice is tender. Stir well, then sprinkle with cilantro and serve.

Per Serving: Calories 284; Fat 8.59g; Sodium 307mg; Carbs 47.3g; Fiber 4.6g; Sugar 4.86g; Protein 5.8g

Coconut Sweet Potatoes Hash

Prep Time: 15 minutes | Cook Time: 5½-7½ hours | Serves: 6

4 sweet potatoes, peeled and cubed
¼ cup brown sugar
¼ cup pineapple juice
½ teaspoon cinnamon
2 tablespoons honey

1 teaspoon salt
⅛ teaspoon pepper
2 tablespoons butter
⅛ cup coconut
½ cup granola

1. Add cubed sweet potatoes, brown sugar, cinnamon, honey, pineapple juice, salt, pepper, and butter to the pot, stir to mix well. Cover and turn the dial to Slow Cook, cook on low heat for 7–9 hours or until potatoes are tender. 2. Using a potato masher, partially mash the potatoes; stir well. In small saucepan over medium heat, toast coconut, stirring frequently, until browned, about 5–7 minutes. Sprinkle over potatoes, then top with granola. 3. Cover and cook on high for 20–30 minutes longer until hot, then serve.

Per Serving: Calories 184; Fat 4.37g; Sodium 481mg; Carbs 35.79g; Fiber 3g; Sugar 20.63g; Protein 1.78g

Creamy Baby Peas and Rice Casserole

Prep Time: 15 minutes | Cook Time: 5½-6½ hours | Serves: 6

1 tablespoon butter
1 onion, chopped
2 cups long grain brown rice
4 cups water
1 teaspoon dried Italian seasoning

⅛ teaspoon pepper
1½ cups frozen baby peas, thawed
½ cup sour cream
¼ cup grated Parmesan cheese

1. Add butter to the pot and turn the dial to Sear/Sauté, set temperature to LO, and press START/STOP to begin cooking. When the butter is melted, add the onion, cook and stir for 4 minutes. Add rice; cook and stir for 3 minutes longer. Press START/STOP to turn off the Sear/Sauté function. 2. Add water, Italian seasoning, and pepper. Cover and turn the dial to Slow Cook, cook on low heat for 5–6 hours or until rice is almost tender. 3. Stir in peas; cover and cook for 30 minutes. Then add sour cream and cheese; cover and cook for 30 minutes longer. Stir and serve right away.

Per Serving: Calories 352; Fat 7.11g; Sodium 171mg; Carbs 61.97g; Fiber 5g; Sugar 1.45g; Protein 10.13g

Sweet and Spicy Peanut Pasta with Celery

Prep Time: 15 minutes | Cook Time: 6 hours | Serves: 4 Nonstick cooking spray

¾ cup honey
2 tablespoons sriracha sauce
1½ tablespoons low-sodium soy sauce or tamari
2 garlic cloves, minced
2 teaspoons dried basil
1 small onion, diced

2 carrots, julienned
1 bell pepper, seeded and diced
2 celery stalks, diced
2 cups peanuts
1-pound uncooked spaghetti

1. Spray the pot generously with nonstick cooking spray. 2. Add the honey, sriracha, garlic, soy sauce, and basil to the pot and blend well. 3. Add the onion, carrots, bell pepper, and celery, and stir to mix well. 4. Cover and turn the dial to Slow Cook, cook on low for about 6 hours. 5. Stir in the peanuts. 6. While the peanuts are warming in the pot, cook the pasta on the stove top according to package instructions. Drain well. 7. Serve the sweet and spicy peanut sauce on top of the cooked spaghetti.

Per Serving: Calories 782; Fat 36.8g; Sodium 304mg; Carbs 101.71g; Fiber 13.3g; Sugar 59.84g; Protein 26.63g

Cheesy Farro and Pea Risotto

Prep Time: 15 minutes | Cook Time: 6-7 hours | Serves: 8

5 cups savory vegetable broth or low-sodium vegetable broth
2 cups whole farro
2 cups frozen peas
1 cup sliced button mushrooms
1 large leek, white and light green parts only, halved and thinly sliced
4 garlic cloves, minced
1 tablespoon extra-virgin olive oil
Freshly ground black pepper
⅓ cup grated Parmesan cheese
½ cup fresh parsley, chopped

1. Add the broth, farro, peas, leek, mushrooms, garlic, olive oil, and pepper to the pot and stir to combine. 2. Cover and turn the dial to Slow Cook, cook on low for 6 to 7 hours, until the farro and vegetables are tender. 3. Stir in the Parmesan cheese and top with the fresh parsley. Serve.

Per Serving: Calories 117; Fat 4.57g; Sodium 209mg; Carbs 14.55g; Fiber 2.3g; Sugar 8.04g; Protein 5.96g

Cheesy Red Potato & Bell Pepper Casserole

Prep Time: 15 minutes | Cook Time: 6 hours | Serves: 6

2½ pounds red potatoes, sliced
4 bell peppers, seeded and diced
2 garlic cloves, minced
1 teaspoon paprika
½ teaspoon salt
½ teaspoon dried oregano
½ teaspoon ground coriander
¼ teaspoon freshly ground black pepper
¾ cup low-sodium vegetable broth
2 cups shredded low-fat Cheddar cheese

1. Add the potatoes, bell peppers, garlic, paprika, salt, oregano, coriander, and pepper to the pot. Pour the broth over the top. 2. Cover and turn the dial to Slow Cook, cook on low for about 6 hours, or until the potatoes are tender. 3. Add the cheese and cook for an additional 30 minutes, or until melted, and serve.

Per Serving: Calories 291; Fat 9.99g; Sodium 591mg; Carbs 35.07g; Fiber 4g; Sugar 5.16g; Protein 17.01g

Maple–Glazed Sweet Potatoes & Pecans

Prep Time: 15 minutes | Cook Time: 6 hours | Serves: 4

4 cups sweet potatoes, cubed
2 tablespoons butter or margarine
¼ cup maple syrup
⅓ cup chopped pecans

1. Add all ingredients to the pot. Cover and turn the dial to Slow Cook, cook on low heat for 6 hours.

Per Serving: Calories 173; Fat 11.72g; Sodium 6mg; Carbs 17.47g; Fiber 2.6g; Sugar 12.24g; Protein 1.69g

Cheesy Carrot

Prep Time: 15 minutes | Cook Time: 7-8 hours | Serves: 8

8 carrots, sliced

1 cup water

2 tablespoons butter

1 (8-ounce) package process American cheese,

cubed

1 (3-ounce) package cream cheese, cubed

1 teaspoon dried thyme leaves

⅓ cup milk

1. Combine carrots, water, and butter in the pot. Cover and turn the dial to Slow Cook, cook on low for 5–6 hours or until carrots are tender. 2. Drain carrots and return to pot. Stir in American cheese, cream cheese, thyme, and milk; mix gently. 3. Cover and cook on low for 2 hours, stirring once during cooking time, until smooth sauce forms. Serve immediately.

Per Serving: Calories 155; Fat 12.91g; Sodium 574mg; Carbs 3.85g; Fiber 0.1g; Sugar 3.28g; Protein 6.18g

Lemon Chickpeas and Wheat Pilaf

Prep Time: 15 minutes | Cook Time: 7-8 hours | Serves: 4

1 cup cracked wheat

1 (15-ounce) can chickpeas, drained

½ teaspoon salt

⅛ teaspoon pepper

2 cups vegetable broth

1 onion, chopped

3 cloves garlic, minced

½ teaspoon grated lemon peel

1 green bell pepper, chopped

1 tablespoon olive oil

½ teaspoon ground cumin

¼ cup lemon juice

⅛ cup chopped parsley

1. Combine all the ingredients except lemon juice and parsley in the pot. Cover and turn the dial to Slow Cook, cook on low for 7–8 hours or until wheat is tender. 2. Add lemon juice and parsley to mixture; stir. Uncover and cook on high for 10–15 minutes or until mixture has thickened slightly. Serve warm.

Per Serving: Calories 289; Fat 7.07g; Sodium 734mg; Carbs 49g; Fiber 9.5g; Sugar 6.66g; Protein 11.42g

Spicy Bean & Rice–Stuffed Bell Peppers

Prep Time: 15 minutes | Cook Time: 7-8 hours | Serves: 6

1 (15-ounce) can no-salt-added black beans, drained and rinsed
1 (15-ounce) can no-salt-added pinto beans, drained and rinsed
1 (4-ounce) can diced green chiles
1¼ cups spicy salsa or store-bought salsa
1 cup frozen corn

1 cup quick-cooking brown rice
1 cup 2% shredded Cheddar cheese, divided
2 teaspoons ground cumin
2 teaspoons chili powder
6 bell peppers (any color), tops cut off, seeded, membrane removed
1 cup water

1. Add the black beans, pinto beans, chiles, salsa, corn, rice, ¾ cup of cheese, cumin, and chili powder to a large bowl and mix well. 2. Fill each bell pepper with the mixture and stand each pepper in the pot, top-side up. Pour the water in the space between the peppers, being careful not to pour it over the peppers or filling. 3. Cover and turn the dial to Slow Cook, cook on low for 7 to 8 hours. 4. Sprinkle each pepper with the remaining ¼ cup of cheese. Cover and cook an additional 3 to 4 minutes, or until cheese is melted. 5. Serve hot.

Per Serving: Calories 219; Fat 9.03g; Sodium 613mg; Carbs 27.09g; Fiber 5.4g; Sugar 6.22g; Protein 10.29g

Lemon–Cheese Risotto

Prep Time: 15 minutes | Cook Time: 5-6 hours | Serves: 6

5 cups chicken stock or low-sodium chicken broth
2 cups short-grain brown rice
1 cup water
4 garlic cloves, minced
4 shallots, minced
1 tablespoon extra-virgin olive oil

1 teaspoon dried thyme
½ cup fresh grated Parmesan cheese
2 teaspoons lemon zest
1 tablespoon freshly squeezed lemon juice
Freshly ground black pepper

1. Add the stock, rice, garlic, shallots, water, olive oil, and thyme to the pot. Stir well. Cover and turn the dial to Slow Cook, cook on low for 5 to 6 hours, until the rice is tender. 2. Stir in the Parmesan cheese, lemon zest, and lemon juice and continue cooking on low for 20 minutes more. Season with the pepper. 3. Serve hot.

Per Serving: Calories 324; Fat 4.9g; Sodium 233mg; Carbs 58.43g; Fiber 2.2g; Sugar 0.92g; Protein 11.03g

Basil Chickpeas and Olives

Prep Time: 15 minutes | Cook Time: 6 hours | Serves: 8

2 (15-ounce) cans chickpeas, drained
1 cup water
2 teaspoons kosher salt
¼ cup extra-virgin olive oil
1 teaspoon black pepper

1 cup fresh basil, chopped
5 cloves garlic, minced
2 tomatoes, diced
½ cup kalamata olives, sliced

1. Add all ingredients to the pot. Cover and turn the dial to Slow Cook, cook on low heat for 6 hours.
Per Serving: Calories 134; Fat 5.65g; Sodium 859mg; Carbs 16.9g; Fiber 4.9g; Sugar 3.38g; Protein 5.08g

Caramelized Onion Rings

Prep Time: 15 minutes | Cook Time: 10 hours | Serves: 4

4 pounds Vidalia or other sweet onions
3 tablespoons butter, thinly sliced

3 tablespoons vegetable oil

1. Peel and slice the onions in ¼" slices. Separate slices into rings. 2. Place the onions into the pot. Scatter butter or margarine slices over top of the onions and drizzle with vegetable oil. Cover and turn the dial to Slow Cook, cook on low for 10 hours. 3. If after 10 hours the onions are wet, turn the pot up to high and cook uncovered for 30 more minutes, or until the liquid evaporates.
Per Serving: Calories 312; Fat 19.2g; Sodium 105mg; Carbs 34.25g; Fiber 4.1g; Sugar 22.78g; Protein 3.72g

Orange–Glazed Carrots with Raisins

Prep Time: 15 minutes | Cook Time: 3-4 hours | Serves: 10

2 tablespoons olive oil, divided
2 pounds fresh baby carrots
¼ packed cup dark brown sugar
1 teaspoon grated fresh ginger (or ½ teaspoon

ground)
½ cup raisins (or dried cranberries)
Juice and zest of 3 large oranges

1. Grease the pot with ½ tablespoon of the olive oil. 2. Place the baby carrots in the bottom of the pot. Stir in brown sugar, ginger, raisins, orange juice and zest and remaining olive oil. 3. Cover and turn the dial to Slow Cook, cook on high for 3–4 hours. If sauce is too liquid, remove cover and cook for another half hour on high. Serve hot.
Per Serving: Calories 77; Fat 2.92g; Sodium 53mg; Carbs 12.69g; Fiber 2.8g; Sugar 7.76g; Protein 0.87g

Chapter 3 Snack and Appetizers

Gingered Teriyaki Mushrooms

Prep Time: 15 minutes | Cook Time: 3 hours | Serves: 4

2 (8-ounce) packages whole cremini mushrooms
½ cup low-sodium soy sauce, tamari, or coconut aminos
¼ cup maple syrup
2 tablespoons rice vinegar
2 garlic cloves, minced

1 piece (1-inch) fresh ginger, peeled and minced, or 1 teaspoon ground ginger
2 tablespoons sesame seeds, divided
2 scallions, green and white parts, chopped, for serving

1. Place the mushrooms in the pot. 2. In a medium bowl, mix together the soy sauce, maple syrup, garlic, rice vinegar, and ginger. 3. Pour the sauce over the mushrooms and sprinkle with 1 tablespoon of sesame seeds. 4. Cover and turn the dial to Slow Cook, cook on High heat for 3 hours or on Low heat for 6 hours. 5. Serve the mushrooms garnished with the scallions and the remaining 1 tablespoon of sesame seeds.
Per Serving: Calories 268; Fat 11.27g; Sodium 1195mg; Carbs 17.47g; Fiber 0.9g; Sugar 12.18g; Protein 24.09g

Hummus and Pickles Salad

Prep Time: 15 minutes | Cook Time: 4 hours | Serves: 4

1 (1-pound) bag dried chickpeas, rinsed and sorted to remove small stones and debris
7 cups water
¼ teaspoon baking soda
5 tablespoons plant-based mayonnaise
1 tablespoon yellow mustard
¼ cup diced dill pickles

¼ cup finely diced onions
1 celery stalk, diced
2 tablespoons rice vinegar
½ teaspoon kelp powder
Ground black pepper
Salt (optional)

1. Add the chickpeas, water, and baking soda to the pot. Cover and turn the dial to Slow Cook, cook on High for 4 hours or on Low for 8 to 9 hours. Strain and discard the liquid. 2. Put 2 cups of the chickpeas that have been cooked into a food processor and pulse them 5 to 10 times so that they are broken up but not completely mashed. After pulsing, move the chickpeas to a medium-sized bowl. Keep the remaining chickpeas for another recipe. 3. Mix together mayonnaise, mustard, celery, pickles, onions, vinegar, kelp powder, pepper, and salt (if desired) in the bowl with the chickpeas that were pulsed. 4. Stir the ingredients well until they form a salad and then refrigerate it until it is ready to be served.
Per Serving: Calories 499; Fat 13g; Sodium 383mg; Carbs 73.66g; Fiber 14.6g; Sugar 12.82g; Protein 24.69g

Spicy Lime Corn

Prep Time: 15 minutes | Cook Time: 6 hours | Serves: 4

4½ cups frozen corn
1 small red onion, diced
1 small green bell pepper, diced
Juice and zest of 2 limes

2 teaspoons chili powder
1 teaspoon ground cumin
1 teaspoon garlic powder
Salt (optional)

1. Add the corn, bell pepper, onion, lime juice and zest, cumin, chili powder, garlic powder, and salt (if using) to the pot. Stir to mix well. 2. Cover and turn the dial to Slow Cook, cook on Low for about 6 hours. 3. Refrigerate the leftovers in an airtight container for 3 to 4 days or freeze for up to 1 month, and reheat in the microwave.

Per Serving: Calories 233; Fat 2.62g; Sodium 48mg; Carbs 47.05g; Fiber 5.3g; Sugar 7.15g; Protein 6.66g

Maple-Orange Kale

Prep Time: 15 minutes | Cook Time: 8 hours | Serves: 4

¼ cup pure maple syrup
1 teaspoon garlic powder
Grated zest and juice of 1 orange
1 teaspoon sea salt

¼ to ½ teaspoon red pepper flakes
¼ teaspoon freshly ground black pepper
2 pounds kale, stems trimmed

1. Mix together the maple syrup, garlic powder, orange zest and juice, red pepper flakes, salt, and pepper in a small bowl. 2. Place the kale in the pot. Add the syrup mixture to the kale, tossing to coat the leaves. 3. Cover and turn the dial to Slow Cook, cook on low for 8 hours; then gently stir the kale and serve.

Per Serving: Calories 175; Fat 2.18g; Sodium 673mg; Carbs 35.95g; Fiber 8.3g; Sugar 18.86g; Protein 10.01g

Maple-Orange Glazed Carrots

Prep Time: 15 minutes | Cook Time: 8 hours | Serves: 6

¼ cup pure maple syrup
½ teaspoon ground ginger
¼ teaspoon ground nutmeg

½ teaspoon sea salt
Juice of 1 orange
1½ pounds baby carrots

1. Combine the maple syrup, ginger, nutmeg, salt, and orange juice in a small bowl, stir to mix well. 2. Place the carrots in the pot. Add the syrup mixture to the carrots, tossing to coat. 3. Cover and turn the dial to Slow Cook, cook on low for 8 hours, until the carrots are very tender.

Per Serving: Calories 81; Fat 0.23g; Sodium 284mg; Carbs 19.8g; Fiber 3.4g; Sugar 14.55g; Protein 0.85g

Parmesan–Garlic Green Beans

Prep Time: 15 minutes | Cook Time: 6 hours | Serves: 6

3 pounds green beans, trimmed

⅓ cup vegetable broth (or store-bought)

4 garlic cloves, minced

⅔ cup shaved Parmesan cheese

½ teaspoon sea salt

¼ teaspoon freshly ground black pepper

1 tablespoon unsalted butter, cut into small pieces

1. Put the green beans in the pot. 2. Pour the broth into the pot. Sprinkle the garlic, Parmesan cheese, salt, and pepper over the green beans. Top with the pieces of butter. 3. Cover and turn the dial to Slow Cook, cook on low for 6 hours or on high for 3 hours, or until the beans are tender.

Per Serving: Calories 112; Fat 5.45g; Sodium 431mg; Carbs 12.24g; Fiber 4.4g; Sugar 1.91g; Protein 5.93g

Honey and Vinegar Glazed Cabbage and Apples

Prep Time: 15 minutes | Cook Time: 8 hours | Serves: 6

¼ cup honey

¼ cup apple cider vinegar

2 tablespoons chili garlic sauce

1 teaspoon grated orange zest

½ teaspoon sea salt

3 sweet-tart apples (such as Braeburn), peeled, cored, and sliced

2 heads green cabbage, cored and shredded

1 red onion, thinly sliced

1. Mix together the honey, chili garlic sauce, vinegar, orange zest, and salt in a small bowl. 2. Place the apples, cabbage, and onion in the pot. Add the honey mixture and stir to coat. 3. Cover and turn the dial to Slow Cook, cook on low for 8 hours, or until the cabbage and apples are tender. Serve.

Per Serving: Calories 96; Fat 0.28g; Sodium 291mg; Carbs 24.84g; Fiber 1.6g; Sugar 21.66g; Protein 0.52g

Buffalo Chicken Wings

Prep Time: 15 minutes | Cook Time: 6 hours | Serves: 6

2 pounds chicken wings

1 (16-ounce) jar buffalo hot sauce

4 tablespoons (½ stick) butter, melted

1. Add the chicken wings, buffalo sauce, and melted butter to the pot, stir to mix well. 2. Cover and turn the dial to Slow Cook, cook on low for 6 hours, until the wings are cooked through. Serve hot.

Per Serving: Calories 283; Fat 13.18g; Sodium 792mg; Carbs 5.81g; Fiber 1.6g; Sugar 3.41g; Protein 34.63g

Simple Baked Chickpeas with Herbs

Prep Time: 15 minutes | Cook Time: 40 minutes | Serves: 4

1½ tablespoons extra-virgin olive oil
2 to 4 teaspoons spices or chopped herbs like chili powder, garlic powder, curry powder, freshly ground black pepper, smoked paprika, chives,

parsley, cilantro, dill
1 (15-ounce) can garbanzo beans, drained and rinsed

1. In a small bowl, whisk the oil and seasonings together, then add the chickpeas and toss to coat. Spread in the pot in a single layer. 2. Cover with the lid and turn the dial to Bake, set the temperature to 350°F, set the time to 40 minutes, press START/STOP to begin cooking. Bake until nicely browned and slightly crispy.

Per Serving: Calories 112; Fat 4.01g; Sodium 218mg; Carbs 15.19g; Fiber 4.5g; Sugar 2.64g; Protein 4.67g

Easy Slow-Cooked Sweet Potatoes

Prep Time: 15 minutes | Cook Time: 8 hours | Serves: 4

4 medium sweet potatoes, scrubbed

1. Wrap each sweet potato in aluminum foil and put them in the pot. 2. Cover and turn the dial to Slow Cook, cook on low for 8 hours. 3. Unwrap to serve.

Per Serving: Calories 115; Fat 0.21g; Sodium 41mg; Carbs 26.76g; Fiber 3.8g; Sugar 8.67g; Protein 2.07g

Chipotle Mayo Glazed Corn

Prep Time: 15 minutes | Cook Time: 10 minutes | Serves: 4

4 ears husked sweet corn
2 tablespoons corn oil
½ cup low-sodium mayonnaise
1 teaspoon chili powder

1 teaspoon garlic powder
½ teaspoon chipotle powder
Freshly ground black pepper
1 lime, quartered

1. Brush the corn with the oil and place in the pot. 2. Cover and turn the dial to Bake. Set the temperature to 380°F and set the time to 10 minutes. Press START/STOP to begin cooking. 3. In the meantime, stir together the mayonnaise, garlic powder, chili powder, chipotle powder, and black pepper. 4. Remove the corn from the pot and brush with the chipotle mayo. 5. Serve with lime quarters to squeeze over the corn.

Per Serving: Calories 257; Fat 14.18g; Sodium 72mg; Carbs 33.55g; Fiber 4.2g; Sugar 6.03g; Protein 4.96g

Cheesy Chicken Enchilada Dip

Prep Time: 15 minutes | Cook Time: 6 hours | Serves: 6

1 tablespoon butter

1-pound chicken tenderloins

1 (15-ounce) can red enchilada sauce

½ tablespoon minced garlic

½ teaspoon chipotle powder

8 ounces cream cheese, cut into 1-inch pieces

1 cup shredded cheddar cheese

Freshly ground black pepper

4 scallions, thinly sliced

Tortilla chips, for serving

1. Coat the inside of the pot with the butter, making sure to cover about two-thirds up the sides of the pot. 2. Add the chicken, garlic, enchilada sauce, and chipotle powder to the pot. Stir to mix well. 3. Cover and turn the dial to Slow Cook, cook on low for 6 hours. Using two forks or meat claws, shred the chicken. 4. Add the cream cheese and cheddar to the pot. Stir until well blended. Taste, and add black pepper as desired. 5. Sprinkle with the scallions and serve with tortilla chips.

Per Serving: Calories 331; Fat 22.67g; Sodium 393mg; Carbs 8.28g; Fiber 0.9g; Sugar 3.49g; Protein 23.72g

Creamy Garlic Cauliflower

Prep Time: 15 minutes | Cook Time: 3 hours | Serves: 6

1 head of cauliflower

3 cups water

4 garlic cloves

1 shallot

1 bay leaf

1 tablespoon extra-virgin olive oil

1 to 2 tablespoons milk

Freshly ground black pepper

¼ cup freshly chives

1. Cut the cauliflower into florets and place them in the pot. 2. Add the water, shallot, garlic, and bay leaf. 3. Cover and turn the dial to Slow Cook, cook on high for 3 hours, or on low for 6 hours. 4. Drain the water. Throw away the garlic cloves, shallot, and bay leaf. 5. Add the olive oil and mix it. 6. Use a potato masher or immersion blender to make the cauliflower creamy. Gradually add milk until you get the consistency you want. 7. Add black pepper for taste and serve with chives on top.

Per Serving: Calories 62; Fat 2.76g; Sodium 46mg; Carbs 8.21g; Fiber 3g; Sugar 2.97g; Protein 2.99g

Delicious Chicken Lettuce Wraps

Prep Time: 15 minutes | Cook Time: 3 hours | Serves: 8

For the Chicken:
2 pounds boneless skinless chicken thighs, roughly chopped
1 tablespoon minced ginger
1 tablespoon minced garlic
Pinch red pepper flakes

1 tablespoon fish sauce (optional)
2 tablespoons soy sauce, gluten-free if desired
1 tablespoon toasted sesame oil
Sea salt
Freshly ground black pepper

For the Lettuce Wraps:
1 head butter lettuce
Handful fresh cilantro, roughly chopped

1 carrot, grated
2 limes, cut into wedges

To Make the Chicken: 1. Place the chicken, ginger, red pepper flakes, garlic, fish sauce (if using), soy sauce, and sesame oil into the pot. Stir to mix well. Season with salt and black pepper. 2. Cover and turn the dial to Slow Cook, cook on high for 3 hours or until the chicken is cooked through.
To assemble the lettuce wraps: 1. Place a spoonful of the chicken mixture in the center of a lettuce leaf. 2. Top with a pinch of cilantro and grated carrot and finish with a squeeze of lime juice.
Per Serving: Calories 176; Fat 5.49g; Sodium 586mg; Carbs 4.21g; Fiber 0.7g; Sugar 1.9g; Protein 26.5g

Sweet-and-Spicy Meatballs with Pineapple

Prep Time: 15 minutes | Cook Time: 6 hours | Serves: 6

1 (12-ounce) bottle chili sauce
1 (12-ounce) jar grape jelly

1 (15-ounce) can pineapple chunks, undrained
2 pounds frozen meatballs, thawed

1. Add the chili sauce, grape jelly, and the juice from the canned pineapple to the pot, stir to mix well. 2. Add the pineapple chunks and meatballs. Stir very gently to coat the meatballs in the sauce. 3. Cover and turn the dial to Slow Cook, cook on low for about 6 hours, until the meatballs are cooked through. Serve hot.
Per Serving: Calories 569; Fat 14.37g; Sodium 1595mg; Carbs 78.91g; Fiber 16.4g; Sugar 47.91g; Protein 35.71g

Garlicky Mashed Potatoes

Prep Time: 15 minutes | Cook Time: 3-4 hours | Serves: 6

6 russet potatoes (about 3 pounds), peeled
1 cup low-sodium vegetable broth or store-bought
1 cup unsweetened plant-based milk, plus more for mashing

5 to 6 garlic cloves, minced
Ground black pepper
Salt (optional)

1. Chop the potatoes into 1- to 2-inch cubes. Put the potatoes in the pot. Pour in the broth. 2. Cover and turn the dial to Slow Cook, cook on High for 3 to 4 hours or on Low for 8 hours, until the potatoes are very soft and easily mashed. 3. Add the milk and garlic, then mash until the texture reaches your desired consistency. 4. If you prefer a smoother consistency, you may need to add up to ½ cup more milk. Add salt and pepper to taste and serve.

Per Serving: Calories 329; Fat 1.79g; Sodium 60mg; Carbs 71.32g; Fiber 5.2g; Sugar 5.56g; Protein 9.76g

Sweet & Sour Butternut Squash and Brussels Sprouts

Prep Time: 15 minutes | Cook Time: 3 hours | Serves: 6

1 medium butternut squash (about 2 to 3 pounds), peeled, seeded, and cut into 1-inch cubes
¾ pound Brussels sprouts, halved
¼ cup apple cider vinegar
2 tablespoons maple syrup

½ teaspoon ground cinnamon
Ground black pepper
Salt (optional)
1 cup chopped pecans
4 to 5 Medjool dates, pitted and chopped

1. Add the butternut squash and Brussels sprouts to the pot. Cover and turn the dial to Slow Cook, cook on High for 3 hours or on Low for 6 hours, checking for doneness each hour, until the squash is tender but not mushy and the Brussels sprouts still have some texture. 2. Prepare the glaze by combining vinegar, maple syrup, and cinnamon in a measuring cup or medium bowl. Pour this mixture over the vegetables and stir gently to cover them. Add salt and pepper to taste. 3. Finally, add pecans and dates, toss everything together, and serve right away.

Per Serving: Calories 212; Fat 12.16g; Sodium 16mg; Carbs 26.51g; Fiber 5.4g; Sugar 18.29g; Protein 4.18g

Classic Hummus

Prep Time: 15 minutes | Cook Time: 0 minutes | Serves: 6

¼ cup tahini, well-stirred
¼ cup freshly squeezed lemon juice
2 tablespoons extra-virgin olive oil, plus more for garnish
2 small garlic cloves, minced
1 teaspoon cumin

⅛ teaspoon freshly ground black pepper
1 (15-ounce) can garbanzo beans (chickpeas), drained and rinsed
2 to 3 tablespoons water
½ teaspoon ground paprika, for garnish

1. Combine the tahini and lemon juice in a food processor and process for one minute. After that, add olive oil, cumin, garlic, and black pepper to the mixture and process for 30 seconds. 2. Then, add half of the chickpeas and process for 1 minute before adding the remaining chickpeas and processing until it becomes thick and smooth for about 1 to 2 minutes. 3. If the mixture is too thick, add 2 to 3 tablespoons of water while the food processor is running until you reach the desired consistency. 4. Finally, serve the hummus with a drizzle of olive oil and paprika.

Per Serving: Calories 164; Fat 11.09g; Sodium 102mg; Carbs 13.13g; Fiber 3.8g; Sugar 2.04g; Protein 4.88g

Rosemary Bakes Potatoes and Beets

Prep Time: 15 minutes | Cook Time: 45 minutes | Serves: 8

Cooking spray
1 pound Yukon gold potatoes, cut into 1-inch pieces
4 medium zucchini, cut into 1-inch pieces
4 carrots, peeled and cut into 1-inch pieces
1 red bell pepper, cut into 1-inch pieces
1 large Vidalia onion, cut into 1-inch pieces

6 to 8 garlic cloves
3 tablespoons extra-virgin olive oil, divided
½ teaspoon freshly ground black pepper, divided
2 tablespoons chopped fresh rosemary, divided
2 medium beets, peeled and cut into 1-inch pieces
2 sprigs fresh rosemary, for garnish (optional)

1. Lightly coat the inside of the pot with the cooking spray. 2. In a large bowl, stir together the potatoes, carrots, zucchini, bell pepper, onion, and garlic. Drizzle 2 tablespoons of the olive oil and season with ¼ teaspoon of the black pepper, and 1½ tablespoons of the chopped rosemary. Stir to combine. 3. Place beets in a medium bowl. Drizzle the remaining 1 tablespoon of olive oil over the beets and season with the remaining ¼ teaspoon black pepper and ½ tablespoon chopped rosemary. Stir to combine. 4. Divide the vegetables evenly inside the pot. 5. Turn dial to Bake, set temperature to 400°F, set the time to 20 minutes and press START/STOP to begin cooking. Gently stir the vegetables halfway through the cooking time. Bake until the vegetables are tender when pierced with a fork and golden brown in some spots, 20 to 25 minutes more. 6. Serve garnished with the rosemary sprigs (if using).

Per Serving: Calories 96; Fat 2.48g; Sodium 80mg; Carbs 17.1g; Fiber 3.1g; Sugar 3.74g; Protein 2.3g

Garlic Spaghetti Squash with Cheese

Prep Time: 15 minutes | Cook Time: 8 hours | Serves: 6

1 spaghetti squash
¼ cup water
¼ cup olive oil

2 garlic cloves, minced
¼ cup low-fat grated Parmesan cheese

1. Prick the spaghetti squash all over with a fork. 2. Put the squash in the pot and add the water. 3. Cover and turn the dial to Slow Cook, cook on low for 8 hours. 4. Allow the squash to cool slightly. When it is cool enough to handle, cut the squash in half. 5. Scrape a fork across the squash flesh to make strands. 6. In a small sauté pan over medium high heat, heat the olive oil. 7. Add the garlic and cook for 30 seconds. 8. Toss the spaghetti squash with the garlic and olive oil mixture and the Parmesan cheese.

Per Serving: Calories 103; Fat 10.25g; Sodium 44mg; Carbs 1.46g; Fiber 0.4g; Sugar 0.76g; Protein 2.01g

Pineapple Turkey Meatballs

Prep Time: 15 minutes | Cook Time: 8 hours | Serves: 6

1-pound ground turkey breast
½ cup whole-wheat bread crumbs
1 onion, grated
1 egg, beaten
1 teaspoon sea salt, divided
¼ teaspoon freshly ground black pepper

1 (8-ounce) can pineapple chunks (no sugar added), with its juice
¼ cup apple cider vinegar
2 tablespoons honey
1 tablespoon cornstarch

1. Mix together the ground turkey, bread crumbs, onion, egg, ½ teaspoon of salt, and the pepper in a medium bowl. 2. Use a small scoop to form the mixture into meatballs. Place the meatballs in your pot. 3. In a small bowl, mix together the juice from the canned pineapple (reserve the pineapple chunks), honey, vinegar, cornstarch, and remaining ½ teaspoon of salt. 4. Add the mixture to the pot, then add the pineapple chunks. 5. Cover and cook on low for 8 hours.

Per Serving: Calories 310; Fat 8.19g; Sodium 739mg; Carbs 34.8g; Fiber 2.7g; Sugar 17.72g; Protein 23.42g

Asian Turkey Meatballs

Prep Time: 15 minutes | Cook Time: 8 hours | Serves: 6

1-pound ground turkey
6 garlic cloves, minced
6 scallions, minced
1 tablespoon grated fresh ginger
¼ cup chopped fresh cilantro

1 egg, beaten
2 tablespoons low-sodium soy sauce
½ teaspoon sesame-chili oil
¼ cup poultry broth, or store bought

1. Mix together the ground turkey, garlic, egg, scallions, ginger, cilantro, soy sauce, and sesame-chili oil in a medium bowl. 2. Using a small scoop, form the mixture into balls. Put the meatballs in the pot. Add the broth. 3. Cover and turn the dial to Slow Cook. cook on low for 8 hours.

Per Serving: Calories 411; Fat 35.88g; Sodium 225mg; Carbs 4.65g; Fiber 0.9g; Sugar 0.59g; Protein 17.09g

Hot Chicken Wings with Blue Cheese Dip

Prep Time: 15 minutes | Cook Time: 8 hours | Serves: 6

1 cup Louisiana hot sauce
2 tablespoons olive oil
½ teaspoon cayenne pepper
2 pounds chicken wings
¼ cup fat-free sour cream

¼ cup fat-free mayonnaise
¼ cup blue cheese crumbles
1 tablespoon Dijon mustard
1 teaspoon low-sodium Worcestershire sauce
3 celery stalks, cut into sticks

1. Mix together the hot sauce, olive oil, and cayenne in a small bowl. Pour the mixture into the pot. 2. Add the chicken wings and toss to coat. 3. Cover and turn the dial to Slow Cook, cook on low for 8 hours. 4. In a small bowl, combine the sour cream, mayonnaise, blue cheese crumbles, Dijon mustard, and Worcestershire sauce, stir to mix well. 5. Serve the chicken wings and celery sticks with the blue cheese mixture on the side for dipping.

Per Serving: Calories 268; Fat 11.35g; Sodium 1231mg; Carbs 4.46g; Fiber 0.8g; Sugar 1.34g; Protein 35.07g

Rice Cereal and Peanuts Party Mix

Prep Time: 15 minutes | Cook Time: 6 hours | Serves: 12

8 cups rice cereal, gluten-free if desired

2 cups pretzels or pretzel sticks, gluten-free if desired

1 cup roasted unsalted peanuts

6 tablespoons (¾ stick) butter, melted

3 tablespoons Worcestershire sauce

2 teaspoons sea salt

Pinch cayenne pepper

½ tsp garlic powder

½ tsp onion powder

1. Add the cereal, pretzels, and peanuts to the pot, stir to mix well. 2. In a medium bowl, mix together the butter, Worcestershire sauce, cayenne, onion powder, salt, and garlic powder. Pour the butter mixture over the cereal mixture and stir well to mix. 3. Cover and turn the dial to Slow Cook, cook on low for 6 hours, stirring about every 45 minutes to make sure it doesn't burn. 4. Spread the mixture out onto a large baking sheet and let it cool to room temperature. 5. Store in a covered container at room temperature for up to 1 week.

Per Serving: Calories 497; Fat 33.83g; Sodium 587mg; Carbs 58.28g; Fiber 18g; Sugar 3.47g; Protein 16.96g

Cheese Spinach–Artichoke Dip

Prep Time: 15 minutes | Cook Time: 6 hours | Serves: 6

1 tablespoon butter

1 (8-ounce) bag frozen spinach, thawed

1 (12-ounce) jar quartered artichoke hearts, drained

2 garlic cloves, minced

4 scallions, thinly sliced

8 ounces cream cheese, cut into 1-inch pieces

1 cup sour cream

1 cup shredded mozzarella cheese

1 cup grated Parmesan cheese (not the canned stuff)

Freshly ground black pepper

Cut up assorted vegetables, for serving

Sliced baguette, for serving

1. Coat the inside of the pot with the butter, making sure to cover about two-thirds up the sides of the pot. 2. Squeeze as much of the extra liquid from the spinach as possible until you have a small amount left. Combine it in a pot with artichoke hearts, garlic, scallions, cream cheese, sour cream, mozzarella, and Parmesan, and mix together carefully. 3. Cover and turn the dial to Slow Cook, cook on low for about 6 hours, or until the cheese is melted. Stir, taste, and add black pepper as desired. 4. Serve with the vegetables and sliced baguette.

Per Serving: Calories 299; Fat 21.68g; Sodium 685mg; Carbs 11.38g; Fiber 3g; Sugar 2.17g; Protein 16.45g

Chapter 4 Soup, Salad and Stew

Cheesy Broccoli Soup

Prep Time: 15 minutes | Cook Time: 6-8 hours | Serves: 6

1 tablespoons butter
1 tablespoon olive oil
1 onion, chopped
2 cloves garlic, minced
⅛ teaspoon pepper
½ teaspoon dried basil leaves

1 (10-ounce) package frozen cut broccoli
3 cups chicken stock
1 (10-ounce) can condensed Cheddar cheese soup
2 cups milk
1 (3-ounce) package cream cheese, cubed
1 cup diced process American cheese

1. Add butter and olive oil to the pot. Turn dial to Sear/Sauté, set temperature to HI, and press START/STOP to begin cooking. When the butter is melted, add the onions and garlic. Cook, uncovered, for 30 minutes. Press START/STOP button to turn off the Sear/Sauté function. 2. Stir onions and garlic, then add pepper, basil, broccoli, stock, and soup. Stir well, then cover and turn the dial to Slow Cook, cook on low for 5–6 hours or until broccoli is very tender. 3. Turn off pot. Using an immersion blender or potato masher, purée the broccoli in the soup. Stir in remaining ingredients. 4. Cover and cook on low for 1–2 hours or until cheese melts and soup is hot. Stir to combine, then serve immediately.

Per Serving: Calories 350; Fat 23.3g; Sodium 1292mg; Carbs 21.05g; Fiber 2.7g; Sugar 12.29g; Protein 15.52g

Creamy Pumpkin Soup

Prep Time: 15 minutes | Cook Time: 5½-6½ hours | Serves: 4

1 (15-ounce) can solid-pack pumpkin
1 onion, chopped
2 cloves garlic, minced
1 teaspoon ground ginger
4 cups chicken stock
1 cup water

1 teaspoon salt
¼ teaspoon white pepper
½ teaspoon dried marjoram leaves
½ cup heavy cream
¼ cup sour cream
2 tablespoons cornstarch

1. Add the pumpkin, onions, garlic, and ginger to the pot; stir to mix well. Gradually stir in stock, stirring with wire whisk until blended. 2. Add water, salt, pepper, and marjoram. Stir to combine. Cover and turn the dial to Slow Cook, cook on low heat for 5–6 hours or until soup is hot and blended. 3. In medium bowl combine heavy cream, sour cream, and cornstarch; mix well. Stir into soup, cover with the lid, and cook on high heat for 30 minutes or until soup is hot.

Per Serving: Calories 322; Fat 15.84g; Sodium 951mg; Carbs 33.22g; Fiber 6.2g; Sugar 5.44g; Protein 12.9g

Cheese Chicken Corn Soup

Prep Time: 15 minutes | Cook Time: 7-8 hours | Serves: 6

2 tablespoons butter
1 tablespoon vegetable oil
1 onion, chopped
3 cloves garlic, minced
2 boneless, skinless chicken breasts, cubed
1 (10.75-ounce) can cream of chicken soup
2 cups chicken stock

3 cups water
½ teaspoon dried basil leaves
⅛ teaspoon pepper
1 cup frozen corn
1 (15-ounce) can cream-style corn
1 cup shredded Swiss cheese

1. Add butter and oil to the pot. Turn dial to Sear/Sauté, set temperature to LO, and press START/STOP to begin cooking. Once the butter is melted, add onion and garlic; cook and stir until crisp-tender, about 5 minutes. Press START/STOP to turn off the Sear/Sauté function. 2. Add remaining ingredients except cheese to the pot. Keep cheese refrigerated until ready to serve. Stir to blend. 3. Cover and turn the dial to Slow Cook, cook on low for 7–8 hours or until chicken is thoroughly cooked and soup is blended. Stir in cheese until melted, and serve.

Per Serving: Calories 365; Fat 17.23g; Sodium 765mg; Carbs 29.14g; Fiber 3.5g; Sugar 3.19g; Protein 24.78g

Curried Chicken, Carrot and Noodle Soup

Prep Time: 15 minutes | Cook Time: 6½ hours | Serves: 4

2 tablespoons butter
1 tablespoon olive oil
2 boneless, skinless chicken breasts
½ teaspoon salt
⅛ teaspoon pepper
2 tablespoons curry powder

1 onion, chopped
3 carrots, sliced
4 cups chicken stock
2 cups water
2 cups egg noodles

1. Sprinkle chicken with salt, pepper, and 1 tablespoon curry powder. Add butter and oil to the pot. Turn dial to Sear/Sauté, set temperature to HI, and press START/STOP to begin cooking. Once the butter is melted, add the chicken to the pot; cook, turning once, for 4–5 minutes or until chicken begins to brown. 2. Remove chicken from the pot. Add onions to the pot; cook and stir until crisp-tender, around 5 minutes; remove from the pot. Press START/STOP to turn off the Sear/Sauté function. 3. Place carrots in the pot. Add onions and chicken to it along with 1 tablespoon curry powder. Pour stock and water over all. 4. Cover and turn the dial to Slow Cook, cook on low for about 6 hours or until chicken and vegetables are tender. Remove chicken from pot and shred. Return chicken to pot; add noodles and stir. 5. Turn heat to high and cook for 15–20 minutes or until noodles are tender. Serve in warmed bowls, topped with minced green onion if desired.

Per Serving: Calories 401; Fat 16.52g; Sodium 1001mg; Carbs 33.29g; Fiber 3.2g; Sugar 5.55g; Protein 29.52g

Beer Cheese Carrot Soup

Prep Time: 15 minutes | Cook Time: 8-9 hours | Serves: 6

1 onion, chopped
2 carrots, chopped
3 cloves garlic, minced
1 teaspoon dried thyme leaves
½ teaspoon salt
⅛ teaspoon pepper
1 (16-ounce) bottle beer

3 cups chicken stock
2 cups milk
2 cups shredded sharp Cheddar cheese
2 tablespoons cornstarch
¼ cup grated Parmesan cheese
3 cups popped popcorn

1. Add onion, carrots, garlic, thyme, salt, pepper, beer, and chicken stock to the pot, stir to mix well. Cover and turn the dial to Slow Cook, cook on low for 8–9 hours. 2. Add milk to pot; cook on low for 1 hour. In medium bowl, mix Cheddar cheese with cornstarch and toss to coat. 3. Add to the pot, cover, and cook on high for 20–25 minutes or until cheese is melted and soup is thickened. Stir in Parmesan cheese, then serve with popcorn.

Per Serving: Calories 312; Fat 19.2g; Sodium 735mg; Carbs 18.24g; Fiber 1.4g; Sugar 7.94g; Protein 16.71g

Wild Rice and Grape Tomato Salad

Prep Time: 15 minutes | Cook Time: 3-4 hours | Serves: 5

1 cup wild rice
½ cup brown rice
1 onion, chopped
2 cups water
1 cup apple juice
½ teaspoon salt
⅛ teaspoon pepper

½ teaspoon dried thyme leaves
½ cup mayonnaise
½ cup sour cream
2 tablespoons tarragon vinegar
1 tablespoon sugar
1 red bell pepper, chopped
½ pint grape tomatoes

1. Add wild rice, brown rice, onions, water, and apple juice to the pot, stir well. Add salt, pepper, and thyme; stir. 2. Cover and turn the dial to Slow Cook, cook on high heat for 3–4 hours or until liquid is absorbed and the rice is tender. 3. Add mayonnaise, sour cream, tarragon vinegar, and sugar to a large bowl; mix well. Add bell peppers and tomatoes. 4. Drain rice mixture if any liquid remains, and stir into mayonnaise mixture. Cover and chill for 3–4 hours. Stir gently before serving.

Per Serving: Calories 335; Fat 11.09g; Sodium 447mg; Carbs 51g; Fiber 3.6g; Sugar 9.12g; Protein 8.91g

Mayo Chicken and Grapes Salad

Prep Time: 15 minutes | Cook Time: 0 minutes | Serves: 4

2 pot simmered chicken breasts, cubed
1 cup seedless red grapes, cut in half
3 stalks celery, chopped
½ cup golden raisins
¼ cup dark raisins
½ cup mayonnaise

¼ cup vanilla yogurt
¼ teaspoon salt
⅛ teaspoon white pepper
½ teaspoon paprika
¼ cup heavy whipping cream

1. Add the cubed chicken breasts, celery, grapes, golden and dark raisins to a large bowl; toss gently. 2. In a medium bowl, mix together the yogurt, mayonnaise, salt, pepper, and paprika. In a bowl, beat the cream until stiff peaks form. Fold into the mayonnaise mixture. 3. Fold mayonnaise mixture into chicken mixture. Cover and chill for 1–2 hours.

Per Serving: Calories 369; Fat 15.79g; Sodium 467mg; Carbs 27.09g; Fiber 1.8g; Sugar 20.85g; Protein 30.48g

Southwest Potato and Corn Salad

Prep Time: 15 minutes | Cook Time: 8-9 hours | Serves: 6

4 russet potatoes
1 onion, chopped
3 cloves garlic, minced
1 jalapeño pepper, minced
1 tablespoon chili powder
½ teaspoon salt
⅛ teaspoon pepper

1 cup water
½ cup mayonnaise
½ cup plain yogurt
⅛ teaspoon cayenne pepper
¼ cup salsa
1½ cups frozen corn, thawed
1 cup cherry tomatoes

1. Peel potatoes and cut into cubes. Place the potatoes to the pot along with the onions, garlic, and jalapeños. Sprinkle with chili powder, salt, and pepper; then pour the water into the pot. 2. Cover and turn the dial to Slow Cook, cook on low for 8–9 hours or until potatoes are tender. Drain potato mixture. 3. In large bowl, mix together the mayonnaise, yogurt, pepper, and salsa. Add hot potato mixture, corn, and tomatoes and stir gently to coat. 4. Cover and chill for 5–6 hours until cold. Stir gently before serving.

Per Serving: Calories 352; Fat 8.02g; Sodium 491mg; Carbs 63.19g; Fiber 5.9g; Sugar 8.67g; Protein 9.57g

Eggplant and Artichokes Stew

Prep Time: 15 minutes | Cook Time: 4-6 hours | Serves: 6

2 tablespoons extra-virgin olive oil
4 garlic cloves, chopped
1 red onion, chopped
1 red bell pepper, seeded and chopped
1 eggplant, chopped
1 (15-ounce) can artichokes, drained and chopped
⅓ cup kalamata olives, pitted and chopped

2 (15-ounce) cans diced tomatoes
4 cups vegetable broth
1 teaspoon red pepper flakes
½ teaspoon dried oregano
½ teaspoon dried parsley
1 teaspoon salt
½ teaspoon pepper

1. Add all ingredients to the pot. Cover and turn the dial to Slow Cook, cook on low heat for 4–6 hours.
Per Serving: Calories 176; Fat 6.43g; Sodium 1158mg; Carbs 27.59g; Fiber 10.5g; Sugar 10.98g; Protein 6.26g

Beef Brisket Stew with Pearl Barley and Celery

Prep Time: 15 minutes | Cook Time: 8 hours | Serves: 2

¼ cup dry pearl barley
½ cup water
½ teaspoon ground cinnamon
½ teaspoon ground coriander
Freshly ground black pepper
⅛ teaspoon sea salt
1 tablespoon tomato paste

¼ cup red wine vinegar
1 cup dry red wine
12 ounces beef brisket, cut into 1-inch cubes
½ cup minced onions
¼ cup minced celery
2 garlic cloves, minced
2 tablespoons minced fresh flat-leaf parsley

1. Add the pearl barley and water to the pot and stir to make sure all the barley is submerged. 2. In a large bowl, mix together the cinnamon, coriander, tomato paste, salt, a few grinds of the black pepper, vinegar, and red wine. 3. Add the beef, onions, garlic, celery, and parsley to the bowl and stir to mix well. Gently pour this mixture over the barley. Do not stir. 4. Cover and turn the dial to Slow Cook, cook on low for 8 hours.
Per Serving: Calories 481; Fat 25.78g; Sodium 1259mg; Carbs 26.41g; Fiber 5.5g; Sugar 2.64g; Protein 28.59g

Chicken and Chickpea Stew

Prep Time: 15 minutes | Cook Time: 5-7 hours | Serves: 6

1 pound boneless, skinless chicken thighs
½ pound dry chickpeas, soaked overnight
5 cups low-sodium chicken broth
1 (15-ounce) can no-salt-added diced tomatoes
1 onion, diced
4 garlic cloves, minced
1 teaspoon ground ginger
1 teaspoon ground cumin
1 teaspoon ground turmeric

1 teaspoon paprika
1 teaspoon red pepper flakes
1 teaspoon ground cinnamon
1 teaspoon ground coriander
1 teaspoon ground nutmeg
1 teaspoon ground cloves
½ teaspoon salt
½ teaspoon freshly ground black pepper
¼ cup chopped fresh cilantro or parsley

1. Add the chicken, chickpeas, broth, tomatoes, onion, cumin, turmeric, paprika, garlic, ginger, red pepper flakes, coriander, cloves, cinnamon, nutmeg, salt, and pepper to the pot. Stir to mix well. 2. Cover and turn the dial to Slow Cook, cook on low for 5 to 7 hours. 3. Top with the cilantro and serve.
Per Serving: Calories 286; Fat 10.13g; Sodium 560mg; Carbs 35.57g; Fiber 6.8g; Sugar 9.01g; Protein 15.6g

Lemon Chickpea, Kale, and Lentil Stew

Prep Time: 15 minutes | Cook Time: 3-4 hours | Serves: 6

1 medium onion, diced
2 celery stalks, diced
5 garlic cloves, minced
4 ounces kale (about 5 or 6 large leaves), chopped
½ cup chopped fresh parsley, divided
1 (1-inch) piece fresh ginger, peeled and minced, or 2 teaspoons ground ginger
1 (14.5-ounce) can chickpeas, drained and rinsed
1 cup dried brown or green lentils, rinsed and sorted
1 (28-ounce) can no-salt-added crushed tomatoes

7 cups low-sodium vegetable broth or store-bought
2 teaspoons paprika
1 teaspoon ground coriander
1 teaspoon ground cumin
½ teaspoon ground cinnamon
¼ teaspoon red pepper flakes
Ground black pepper
Salt (optional)
Juice from ½ lemon

1. Add the onion, celery, garlic, kale, the ginger, chickpeas, lentils, ¼ cup of parsley, paprika, tomatoes, broth, cumin, coriander, cinnamon, red pepper flakes, black pepper, and salt (if using) to the pot. 2. Cover and turn the dial to Slow Cook, cook on High for 3 to 4 hours or on Low for 6 to 8 hours. 3. Stir in the remaining ¼ cup of parsley and the lemon juice. Serve.
Per Serving: Calories 201; Fat 3.62g; Sodium 336mg; Carbs 38.12g; Fiber 9.3g; Sugar 15.41g; Protein 9.2g

Chicken, Shrimp and Vegetables Gumbo

Prep Time: 15 minutes | Cook Time: 6-8 hours | Serves: 8

2 to 3 pounds skinless, boneless chicken thighs
½ pound breakfast sausage
1 bell pepper, seeded and diced
1 onion, diced
2 celery stalks, finely chopped
4 garlic cloves
2 dried bay leaves
1 cup frozen okra
¾ cup no-salt-added tomato paste

1 (15-ounce) can no-salt-added diced tomatoes
1 tablespoon plus 1 teaspoon homemade cajun blend
½ teaspoon freshly ground black pepper
½ teaspoon ground cayenne pepper
½ teaspoon dried thyme
½ teaspoon dried oregano
1-pound raw shrimp, peeled and deveined

1. Add the chicken, sausage, bell pepper, celery, garlic, onion, okra, bay leaves, tomato paste, tomatoes and their juices, cayenne pepper, Cajun blend, black pepper, thyme, and oregano to the pot. Stir to mix well. 2. Cover and turn the dial to Slow Cook, cook on low heat for 6 to 8 hours. 3. Gently stir in the shrimp. Cover with the lid and cook for about 10 to 15 minutes more, or until the shrimp are pink and cooked through. 4. Remove the bay leaves before serving.

Per Serving: Calories 245; Fat 8.29g; Sodium 744mg; Carbs 21.82g; Fiber 3g; Sugar 16.86g; Protein 20.89g

Pork and Potato Stew

2½ pounds boneless pork shoulder, fat trimmed, cut into 1-inch cubes
1 cup cider
2 cups no-salt-added beef broth
½ pound red or yellow potatoes, chopped
2 carrots, chopped
3 celery stalks, chopped
1 large apple, cored and chopped

1 onion, diced
½ tablespoon Dijon mustard
1 tablespoon apple cider vinegar
1½ teaspoons dried thyme
1 teaspoon dried rosemary
½ teaspoon salt
½ teaspoon freshly ground black pepper

1. Add the pork, cider, broth, potatoes, apple, carrots, celery, mustard, vinegar, onion, thyme, rosemary, salt, and pepper to the pot. Stir to mix well. 2. Cover and turn the dial to Slow Cook, cook on low for 4 to 6 hours, or until both the pork and the potatoes are tender, and serve.

Per Serving: Calories 325; Fat 6.92g; Sodium 342mg; Carbs 17.93g; Fiber 3.7g; Sugar 6.78g; Protein 44.52g

Cumin Beef Stew

Prep Time: 15 minutes | Cook Time: 6-8 hours | Serves: 6

1½ pounds beef stew meat
3 cups beef bone broth
1 onion, diced
1 bell pepper, seeded and diced
½ pound potatoes, diced
3 large carrots, peeled and chopped

2 dried bay leaves
3 garlic cloves, chopped
2 teaspoons ground cumin
½ teaspoon salt
¼ teaspoon freshly ground black pepper
1 bunch cilantro, stemmed and finely chopped

1. Add the stew meat, broth, onion, bell pepper, potatoes, carrots, bay leaves, garlic, cumin, salt, and pepper to the pot. Stir to mix well. 2. Cover and turn the dial to Slow Cook, cook on low for 6 to 8 hours. 3. Discard the bay leaves and garnish with fresh cilantro before serving.

Per Serving: Calories 161; Fat 10.12g; Sodium 968mg; Carbs 15.23g; Fiber 2.9g; Sugar 4.2g; Protein 3.4g

Sweet Potato, Beans, and Lentil Stew

Prep Time: 15 minutes | Cook Time: 3-4 hours | Serves: 6

¼ cup chickpea flour
4 medium sweet potatoes (about 1½ pounds), peeled and cut into 1½-inch cubes
1 medium onion, diced
1 garlic clove, minced
1 (14.5-ounce) can red kidney beans, drained and rinsed
1 cup dried green or brown lentils, rinsed and sorted

4½ cups low-sodium vegetable broth or store-bought
1 cup orange juice (from 2 to 3 oranges)
1 teaspoon dried oregano
½ teaspoon celery seed
Ground black pepper
Salt (optional)

1. Place the chickpea flour and sweet potatoes in a gallon-size resealable bag and shake well to coat. 2. Transfer the floured potatoes to the pot. Add the onion, lentils, garlic, beans, broth, orange juice, celery seed, oregano, and pepper. Season with salt (if using). 3. Cover and turn the dial to Slow Cook, cook on High for 3 to 4 hours or on Low for 7 to 8 hours.

Per Serving: Calories 226; Fat 4.27g; Sodium 190mg; Carbs 42.53g; Fiber 5.3g; Sugar 15.97g; Protein 6.66g

Potato, Cabbage and Beer Stew

Prep Time: 15 minutes | Cook Time: 3-4 hours | Serves: 4

1 medium onion, diced
3 carrots, diced
3 celery stalks, diced
1 parsnip, diced
3 garlic cloves, minced
1 pound whole white button or cremini mushrooms
¼ cup chickpea flour
4 russet potatoes (about 2 pounds), peeled and chopped into 1-inch pieces
4 cups low-sodium vegetable broth or store-bought
1 (10- to 14-ounce can or bottle) Irish stout beer,
such as Guinness
1 tablespoon tomato paste
2 tablespoons plant-based worcestershire sauce or store-bought
1 tablespoon dried thyme
1 bay leaf
Ground black pepper
Salt (optional)
Small head savoy or green cabbage, chopped (about 7 cups)

1. Add the onion, carrots, celery, parsnip, garlic, and mushrooms to the pot, stir to mix well. 2. Place the chickpea flour and potatoes in a gallon-size resealable bag and shake well to coat. Transfer the floured potatoes to the pot. 3. Add the broth, beer, Worcestershire sauce, tomato paste, bay leaf, thyme, pepper, and salt (if using) to the pot. Stir well to combine. Cover and turn the dial to Slow Cook, cook on High for 3 to 4 hours or on Low for 7 to 8 hours, stirring occasionally to avoid sticking. 4. In the final 30 minutes of cooking, remove and discard the bay leaf, add the cabbage, and stir well. Serve right away.
Per Serving: Calories 382; Fat 2.36g; Sodium 295mg; Carbs 83.85g; Fiber 14.2g; Sugar 24.95g; Protein 14.48g

Delicious Beef Barley Soup

Prep Time: 15 minutes | Cook Time: 8 hours | Serves: 2

8 ounces beef stew meat, trimmed of fat and cut into 1-inch cubes
¼ cup pearl barley
1 cup diced onion
1 cup diced carrot
1 teaspoon fresh thyme
½ teaspoon dried oregano
2 cups low-sodium beef stock
⅛ teaspoon sea salt

1. Add all the ingredients to the pot and stir to mix well. 2. Cover and turn the dial to Slow Cook, cook on low for 8 hours. The meat should be tender and the barley soft.
Per Serving: Calories 448; Fat 10.79g; Sodium 352mg; Carbs 54.62g; Fiber 7.1g; Sugar 7.36g; Protein 39.29g

Potato, Mushroom and Carrot Stew

Prep Time: 15 minutes | Cook Time: 3-4 hours | Serves: 6

⅓ cup chickpea flour

4 red potatoes (about 1⅓ pounds), unpeeled and cut into 1-inch chunks

1 large onion, diced

4 carrots, cut into 1-inch chunks

4 celery stalks, cut into 1-inch chunks

1 pound whole white button or cremini mushrooms

6 cups low-sodium vegetable broth or store-bought

2 tablespoons plant-based worcestershire sauce or store-bought

2 tablespoons tomato paste

3 bay leaves

2 teaspoons dried thyme

2 teaspoons garlic powder

Ground black pepper

Salt (optional)

1. Place the chickpea flour and potatoes in a gallon-size resealable bag and shake well to coat. Transfer the floured potatoes to the pot. 2. Add the onion, mushrooms, carrots, celery, broth, tomato paste, Worcestershire sauce, bay leaves, garlic powder, thyme, pepper, and salt (if using) to the pot and stir to combine. 3. Cover and turn the dial to Slow Cook, cook on High for 3 to 4 hours or on Low for 7 to 8 hours, stirring occasionally to prevent the stew from sticking. Remove and discard the bay leaves, serve.

Per Serving: Calories 194; Fat 1.83g; Sodium 237mg; Carbs 40.54g; Fiber 7.3g; Sugar 13.94g; Protein 8.14g

Chapter 5 Poultry mains

Creamy Chicken Divan and Broccoli

Prep Time: 15 minutes | Cook Time: 5-6 hours | Serves: 4

2 cups fresh broccoli florets
2 tablespoons lemon juice
1 onion, chopped
1 (4-ounce) jar sliced
½ cup mushrooms, drained

2 cups chopped cooked chicken
1 (10-ounce) can cream of broccoli soup
½ cup light cream
¾ cup shredded Swiss cheese

1. Toss broccoli with lemon juice. Place in the pot. Top with onions, mushrooms, and chicken. 2. In a medium bowl, mix together the soup with cream and cheese. Pour into the pot. 3. Cover and turn the dial to Slow Cook, cook on low for 5–6 hours or until thoroughly heated. Stir well, then serve.

Per Serving: Calories 488; Fat 26.47g; Sodium 1577mg; Carbs 13.16g; Fiber 2.4g; Sugar 5.91g; Protein 49.02g

Juicy BBQ Chicken Thighs

Prep Time: 15 minutes | Cook Time: 8-10 hours | Serves: 4

2 tablespoons vegetable oil
1 onion, chopped
2 cloves garlic, minced
1 jalapeño pepper, minced
¼ cup orange juice
1 tablespoon low-sodium soy sauce
2 tablespoons apple cider vinegar

2 tablespoons brown sugar
2 tablespoons Dijon mustard
1 (8-ounce) can tomato sauce
1 tablespoon chili powder
¼ teaspoon pepper
6 boneless, skinless, chicken thighs

1. Add oil to the pot. Turn dial to Sear/Sauté, set temperature to LO, and press START/STOP to begin cooking. 2. When the oil is heated, add the garlic and onion; cook and stir until crisp-tender, about 4 minutes. Press START/STOP to turn off the Sear/Sauté function. 3. Add jalapeño, orange juice, soy sauce, mustard, vinegar, brown sugar, tomato sauce, chili powder, and pepper to the pot. 4. Add chicken to the sauce, pushing chicken into the sauce to completely cover. 5. Cover and turn the dial to Slow Cook; cook on low heat for 8–10 hours or until chicken is thoroughly cooked.

Per Serving: Calories 475; Fat 25.36g; Sodium 984mg; Carbs 25.61g; Fiber 3.4g; Sugar 9.15g; Protein 36.48g

Chicken and Apple Stew with Pecans

Prep Time: 15 minutes | Cook Time: 6-7 hours | Serves: 4

4 boneless, skinless chicken breasts
½ teaspoon dried thyme leaves
⅛ teaspoon pepper
½ teaspoon salt
1 onion, sliced
½ cup chicken stock

¼ cup apple juice
¼ cup brown sugar
2 tablespoons butter, melted
2 Granny Smith apples, sliced
⅓ cup chopped pecans

1. Sprinkle the chicken with thyme, pepper, and salt. Place onions in the pot. Top with chicken. 2. In a small bowl, mix together the remaining ingredients except apples and pecans, and pour into the pot. 3. Cover and turn the dial to Slow Cook, cook on low for 5 hours. Then stir in apples; cover and cook for 1–2 hours longer or until chicken is thoroughly cooked and apples are tender. 4. Sprinkle with pecans and serve over hot cooked rice.

Per Serving: Calories 588; Fat 20.64g; Sodium 1465mg; Carbs 29.23g; Fiber 3.3g; Sugar 23.81g; Protein 69.62g

Italian Slow–Cooker Chicken and Green Beans

Prep Time: 15 minutes | Cook Time: 9-10 hours | Serves: 6

2-pounds boneless, skinless chicken thighs
½ cup Italian salad dressing
3 russet potatoes, cut into wedges

3 cloves garlic, chopped
1 onion, chopped
1 (10-ounce) package frozen green beans, thawed

1. Combine chicken with salad dressing in a zipper-lock bag. Place in a large bowl and refrigerate for 6–7 hours. 2. When ready to cook, place potatoes, garlic, and onion in the pot. Pour chicken and salad dressing over all. 3. Cover and turn the dial to Slow Cook, cook on low for 8 hours. Then add green beans to the pot. 4. Cover and cook on low for 1–2 hours longer or until chicken is thoroughly cooked and vegetables are tender.

Per Serving: Calories 475; Fat 12.97g; Sodium 609mg; Carbs 71.41g; Fiber 5.7g; Sugar 12.71g; Protein 18.79g

Spanish Chicken and Brown Rice

Prep Time: 15 minutes | Cook Time: 6-7 hours | Serves: 4

2 boneless, skinless chicken breasts
½ teaspoon paprika
⅛ teaspoon pepper
½ teaspoon salt
1 tablespoon vegetable oil
1 onion, chopped
2 cloves garlic, minced

¾ cup long grain brown rice
1 green bell pepper, chopped
1 cup barbecue sauce
1 (8-ounce) can tomato sauce
1 cup chicken stock
2 tablespoons apple cider vinegar
¼ cup chopped fresh parsley

1. Cut chicken breasts into 1-inch cubes. Sprinkle with paprika, pepper, and salt; mix well. 2. Add vegetable oil to the pot. Turn dial to Sear/Sauté, set temperature to HI, and press START/STOP to begin cooking. 3. Once the oil is hot, add the chicken; cook and stir until chicken starts to brown, about 4–5 minutes. 4. Add onions and garlic to the pot; cook until onion is tender, stirring to remove any drippings, about 5 minutes. 5. Add rice to the pot; cook and stir for 3–4 minutes until coated. Press START/STOP to turn off the Sear/Sauté function. 6. Stir in remaining ingredients except parsley. Cover and turn the dial to Slow Cook, cook on low for 6–7 hours or until the chicken is thoroughly cooked and the rice becomes tender. 7. Stir in parsley and serve.
Per Serving: Calories 671; Fat 21.74g; Sodium 1452mg; Carbs 78.41g; Fiber 4.3g; Sugar 28.71g; Protein 39.26g

Orange–Peanut Chicken

Prep Time: 15 minutes | Cook Time: 7-8 hours | Serves: 4

1¼-pounds boneless, skinless chicken thighs
½ cup chunky peanut butter
3 tablespoons low-sodium soy sauce

¼ cup orange juice
1 onion, chopped
1 chopped jalapeño pepper

1. Cut chicken thighs into 2-inch pieces. Place in the pot. 2. In a bowl, combine together the peanut butter, onion, soy sauce, orange juice, and jalapeños, pour into the pot. 3. Cover and turn the dial to Slow Cook, cook on low heat for 7 to 8 hours. Stir well and serve over hot cooked rice, pasta, or couscous.
Per Serving: Calories 467; Fat 24.77g; Sodium 882mg; Carbs 41.34g; Fiber 4.7g; Sugar 14.21g; Protein 23.14g

White-Wine Braised Chicken and Mushroom

Prep Time: 15 minutes | Cook Time: 8 hours | Serves: 2

1 teaspoon extra-virgin olive oil
2 bone-in, skinless chicken breasts, about 12 ounces each
1 cup blanched pearl onions
6 to 8 button mushrooms, quartered

1 teaspoon minced garlic
1 teaspoon fresh thyme
⅛ teaspoon sea salt
Freshly ground black pepper
1 cup dry white wine

1. Grease the inside of the pot with olive oil. Place the chicken in the pot. The chicken breasts should not stack on top of each other. 2. Spread the onions, mushroom, garlic, and thyme over the chicken. Season with salt and black pepper. Pour in the wine. 3. Cover and turn the dial to Slow Cook, cook on low for 8 hours.
Per Serving: Calories 230; Fat 13.54g; Sodium 1432mg; Carbs 9.64g; Fiber 1.9g; Sugar 3.77g; Protein 18.35g

Herbed Chicken with Beans and Bacon

Prep Time: 15 minutes | Cook Time: 8 hours | Serves: 2

1 cup navy beans, drained and rinsed
1 slice smoked bacon, cut into thin strips
1 small onion, halved and sliced thin
4 garlic cloves, smashed
1 teaspoon herbes de Provence

½ cup low-sodium chicken broth
2 bone-in, skinless chicken thighs, about 8 ounces each
⅛ teaspoon sea salt
Freshly ground black pepper

1. Add the beans, bacon, garlic, onion, herbes de Provence, and broth to the pot and stir well to mix. Place the chicken pieces on top of the beans. Season with salt and black pepper. 2. Cover and turn the dial to Slow Cook, cook on low for 8 hours.
Per Serving: Calories 308; Fat 12.46g; Sodium 467mg; Carbs 33.92g; Fiber 10.3g; Sugar 2.07g; Protein 16.39g

Delicious Chicken & Snap Peas with Cashews

Prep Time: 15 minutes | Cook Time: 6 hours | Serves: 2

16 ounces boneless, skinless chicken breasts, cut into 2-inch pieces

2 cups sugar snap peas, strings removed

1 teaspoon grated fresh ginger

1 teaspoon minced garlic

2 tablespoons low-sodium soy sauce

1 tablespoon ketchup

1 tablespoon rice vinegar

1 teaspoon honey

Pinch red pepper flakes

¼ cup toasted cashews

1 scallion, white and green parts, sliced thin

1. Add the chicken and sugar snap peas to the pot. 2. In a bowl, combine together the ginger, garlic, ketchup, soy sauce, honey, vinegar, and red pepper flakes. Pour the mixture over the chicken and snap peas. 3. Cover and turn the dial to Slow Cook, cook on low for 6 hours. The chicken should be cooked through, and the snap peas should be tender, but not mushy. 4. Stir in the cashews and scallions, serve.

Per Serving: Calories 692; Fat 30.42g; Sodium 1297mg; Carbs 76.51g; Fiber 9.4g; Sugar 21.13g; Protein 30.92g

Basil Turkey with Chestnuts

Prep Time: 15 minutes | Cook Time: 45 minutes| Serves: 8

½ stick lemon-grass, finely sliced

1 tbsp cilantro

1 green chili, finely chopped

1 tbsp coconut oil

¼ cup fresh basil leaves

1 white onion, chopped

1 garlic clove, minced

1 thumb size piece of minced ginger

4oz skinless turkey breasts, sliced

4 cups chicken broth

1 cup canned water chestnuts, drained

2 scallions, chopped

1. Crush the lemon-grass, cilantro, chili, 1 tbsp oil and basil leaves in a blender or pestle and mortar to form a paste. 2. Add 1 tbsp olive oil to the pot. Turn dial to Sear/Sauté, set temperature to HI, and press START/STOP to begin cooking. 3. Once the oil is hot, add the onions, garlic and ginger, sauté until soft. 4. Add the turkey and brown for 4-5 minutes on each side. Add the broth and stir. Then, add the paste and stir. 5. Add the water chestnuts, turn down the heat slightly and allow to simmer for 25-30 minutes or until turkey is thoroughly cooked through. 6. Sprinkle the scallions over the top, serve hot.

Per Serving: Calories 212; Fat 9.79g; Sodium 1045mg; Carbs 18.72g; Fiber 1.8g; Sugar 9.01g; Protein 11.8g

Quinoa, Beans and Turkey Chili

Prep Time: 15 minutes | Cook Time: 6-8 hours | Serves: 6

1 cup uncooked quinoa
1-pound ground turkey
1 (28-ounce) can crushed tomatoes, without salt
1 (10-ounce) can diced tomatoes with green chiles, without salt
1 cup marinara sauce
1 (15-ounce) can red kidney beans, drained and rinsed

1 onion, chopped
3 garlic cloves, minced
2 tablespoons chili powder
½ teaspoon salt
2 teaspoons ground cumin
1½ teaspoons paprika
1 teaspoon dried oregano

1. Add the quinoa, turkey, diced tomatoes and their juices, beans, onion, marinara sauce, garlic, chili powder, paprika, salt, cumin, and oregano to the pot. Stir to mix well. 2. Cover and turn the dial to Slow Cook, cook on low heat for 6 to 8 hours and serve.

Per Serving: Calories 568; Fat 38.91g; Sodium 633mg; Carbs 33.96g; Fiber 8g; Sugar 7.55g; Protein 22.76g

Creamy Chicken Tikka Masala

Prep Time: 15 minutes | Cook Time: 6 hours | Serves: 2

16 ounces boneless, skinless chicken breast
1 cup diced onion
1 cup diced fresh tomatoes
1 teaspoon ground coriander
1 teaspoon ground cumin
1 teaspoon smoked paprika

⅛ teaspoon red pepper flakes
1 teaspoon minced fresh ginger
1 cup low-sodium chicken broth
2 tablespoons heavy cream or coconut cream
¼ cup minced fresh cilantro, for garnish

1. Place the chicken, onion, tomatoes, ginger, coriander, red pepper flakes, cumin, paprika, and chicken broth in the pot. Stir to mix well. 2. Cover and turn the dial to Slow Cook, cook on low for 6 hours, until the chicken is cooked through and the tomatoes and onions are soft. 3. Allow the dish to rest in the pot, uncovered, for 10 minutes, stir in the heavy cream. Garnish with the cilantro.

Per Serving: Calories 512; Fat 19.79g; Sodium 657mg; Carbs 59.13g; Fiber 5.9g; Sugar 17.46g; Protein 25.49g

Lemongrass Turkey & Pak Choy Soup

Prep Time: 15 minutes | Cook Time: 4-6 hours | Serves: 6

½ stick of lemongrass, sliced
1 tbsp. of cilantro
1 red chili, finely chopped
1 tbsp. of coconut oil
1 tbsp. of oregano
1 white onion, chopped
1 garlic clove, minced
1 tbsp. of ground ginger

12oz of skinless turkey breast, diced
½ cup of water
½ cup of low-sodium chicken stock
1 fresh lime, juiced
½ cup of pak choy leaves, shredded
1 cup of canned water chestnuts
2 green onions, chopped

1. Crush the lemongrass, cilantro, chili, coconut oil and oregano in a blender or pestle and mortar to form a paste. 2. Add the coconut oil to the pot. Turn dial to Sear/Sauté, set temperature to HI, and press START/STOP to begin cooking. 3. Once the oil is hot, add the onions, garlic and ginger, sauté until soft. 4. Add the turkey cubes and brown evenly on each side. 5. Add the water and stir. Press START/STOP to turn off the Sear/Sauté function. Then, add the paste and stock to the pot. 6. Squeeze in the lime juice. Cover and turn the dial to Slow Cook, cook on Low for 4-6 hours. Add the pak choy and water chestnuts 20 minutes before serving. 7. Sprinkle the green onion over the top and serve.

Per Serving: Calories 189; Fat 7.29g; Sodium 50mg; Carbs 17.07g; Fiber 3.5g; Sugar 2.09g; Protein 14.25g

Lemony Whole Turkey with Vegetables

Prep Time: 15 minutes | Cook Time: 8-9 hours | Serves: 8

1 (8-pound) turkey, thawed if frozen
1 tablespoon smoked paprika
2 teaspoons salt
¼ teaspoon black pepper
1 lemon, halved

3 cups sliced carrots
2 cups sliced celery
2 cups pre-chopped yellow onion
2 tablespoons jarred minced garlic

1. Pat dry the turkey. Remove the giblets and save for stock or discard. 2. Sprinkle the turkey with the paprika, salt, and pepper and rub into the skin. Place both lemon halves inside the turkey cavity. 3. Add the carrots, celery, onion, and garlic to the pot. Place the turkey on top of the vegetables. 4. Cover and turn the dial to Slow Cook, cook on Low for 8 to 9 hours, or a food thermometer inserted in the center of the turkey registers 165°F. Test in the thigh and breast areas, being careful not to touch bone. 5. Remove the turkey from the pot and place on a serving plate surrounded by the vegetables. Cover with foil and let rest for 15 minutes before slicing to serve. 6. Discard the lemon halves.

Per Serving: Calories 190; Fat 16.31g; Sodium 620mg; Carbs 4.2g; Fiber 1.2g; Sugar 1.61g; Protein 6.58g

Lemon Herbed Turkey Breast with Vegetables

Prep Time: 15 minutes | Cook Time: 6 hours | Serves: 8

1 (4-pound) turkey breast
2 tablespoons lemon juice
1 teaspoon seasoned salt
1 teaspoon smoked paprika
1 teaspoon dried thyme leaves

1 teaspoon dried Italian seasoning
2 pounds baby Yukon Gold potatoes
1 (16-ounce) bag baby carrots
1 (16-ounce) bag frozen pearl onions
1 cup chicken stock or store-bought chicken stock

1. Drizzle the turkey breast with the lemon juice and sprinkle with the salt, paprika, Italian seasoning and thyme; rub the seasonings into the skin. 2. Add the potatoes, carrots, and onions to the pot. Place the turkey breast on top, skin-side up. Pour the stock over the vegetables, not the turkey. 3. Cover and turn the dial to Slow Cook, cook on Low for 6 hours, or until the turkey registers 165°F on a food thermometer. 4. Slice the turkey and serve with the vegetables. 5. Store leftovers covered in the refrigerator for up to 5 days or freeze for up to 3 months.

Per Serving: Calories 217; Fat 5.64g; Sodium 414mg; Carbs 21.75g; Fiber 2.7g; Sugar 1.64g; Protein 19.12g

Thyme Chicken Pot Pie

Prep Time: 15 minutes | Cook Time: 8 hours | Serves: 4

4 boneless, skinless chicken thighs
2 cups diced, peeled Yukon Gold potatoes
2 cups frozen peas
2 cups diced yellow onions
2 cups sliced carrots
2 teaspoons fresh thyme

¼ teaspoon sea salt
Freshly ground black pepper
2 tablespoons all-purpose flour
2 cups chicken stock (or store-bought)
4 biscuits, warmed and split

1. Place the chicken, potatoes, carrots, peas, onions, and thyme in the pot. Season with salt and black pepper. 2. Mix together the flour and stock in a medium bowl. Pour into the pot and stir. 3. Cover and turn the dial to Slow Cook, cook on low for 8 hours, or until the vegetables are tender. 4. Using tongs, remove the chicken from the pot and shred it with two forks. Return the shredded chicken to the pot, stir, and serve spooned over the biscuits.

Per Serving: Calories 613; Fat 25.14g; Sodium 1194mg; Carbs 57.7g; Fiber 5.7g; Sugar 5.9g; Protein 38.19g

Turkey and Cornbread Casserole

Prep Time: 15 minutes | Cook Time: 6 hours | Serves: 4

Nonstick cooking spray
1-pound lean ground turkey
1 poblano chile, seeded and chopped
4 scallions, chopped
2 (15-ounce) cans black beans, drained and rinsed
2 cups fresh or frozen corn
1 large tomato, diced
½ cup chopped fresh cilantro

¼ cup sliced black olives
1 (10-ounce) can enchilada sauce
1 teaspoon ground cumin
½ teaspoon chili powder
¼ teaspoon freshly ground black pepper
1 (8.5-ounce) package cornbread mix, plus ingredients required on package
1 cup grated Colby cheese

1. Spray the pot with nonstick cooking spray. 2. Add the ground turkey to the pot. Turn dial to Sear/Sauté, set temperature to HI, and press START/STOP to begin cooking. Break up the meat with a wooden spoon, for 8 to 10 minutes, until cooked through. Drain if necessary. Press START/STOP to turn off the Sear/Sauté function. 3. Add the poblano chile, scallions, corn, black beans, tomato, olives, cilantro, enchilada sauce, chili powder, cumin, and black pepper to the pot. Stir to mix well. 4. Make the cornbread batter according to the package instructions. Spoon the batter over the meat and bean mixture in the pot. Spread the cheese on top. 5. Cover and turn the dial to Slow Cook, cook on low for 6 hours or on high for 3 hours, until the cornbread springs back to the touch. 6. Serve hot, dishing up both the turkey mixture and the cornbread topping in each serving.

Per Serving: Calories 717; Fat 29.58g; Sodium 1363mg; Carbs 76.2g; Fiber 11.2g; Sugar 20.79g; Protein 39.6g

Cheese Chicken and Bacon Casserole

Prep Time: 15 minutes | Cook Time: 6-8 hours | Serves: 6

3 pounds boneless, skinless chicken thighs
4 slices bacon, cooked and crumbled
8 ounces low-fat cream cheese, cubed
8 ounces low-fat sour cream
8 ounces Cheddar cheese, shredded

¼ cup diced yellow onion
1 teaspoon garlic powder
1 teaspoon dried parsley
½ teaspoon sea salt
¼ teaspoon freshly ground black pepper

1. Place all the ingredients in the pot. Stir to mix well. 2. Cover and turn the dial to Slow Cook, cook on low for 6 for 8 hours or on high for 3 to 4 hours, until the chicken reads 165°F on a food thermometer. 3. Stir and serve.

Per Serving: Calories 713; Fat 42.89g; Sodium 1248mg; Carbs 11.01g; Fiber 0.1g; Sugar 7.39g; Protein 68.19g

Red Wine–Braised Chicken with Tomatoes

Prep Time: 15 minutes | Cook Time: 6 hours | Serves: 4

1 cup dry red wine

1 cup chicken stock (or store-bought)

1 (28-ounce) can plum tomatoes, undrained

1 red bell pepper, seeded and sliced

1 yellow onion, sliced

1 cup sliced button or cremini mushrooms

4 garlic cloves, minced

½ teaspoon sea salt

⅛ teaspoon freshly ground black pepper

8 bone-in chicken thighs, skin removed

1. Add the wine, stock, tomatoes with their juices, mushrooms, bell pepper, onion, and garlic to the pot. Stir to mix well. 2. Sprinkle the chicken with salt and pepper. Arrange the chicken thighs on top of the vegetables. 3. Cover and turn the dial to Slow Cook, cook on low for 6 hours, or until the vegetables are tender and the chicken reads 165°F on a food thermometer.

Per Serving: Calories 283; Fat 13.67g; Sodium 475mg; Carbs 6.58g; Fiber 0.7g; Sugar 4.18g; Protein 29.54g

Honey–Teriyaki Chicken Thighs

Prep Time: 15 minutes | Cook Time: 6-8 hours | Serves: 6

1 (16-ounce) bottle teriyaki sauce

¼ cup honey

4 garlic cloves, minced

Pinch red pepper flakes

2½ pounds bone-in skinless chicken thighs

Steamed white rice, for serving

4 scallions, thinly sliced, for serving

2 tablespoons sesame seeds, for serving

1. Combine the teriyaki sauce, garlic, honey, and red pepper flakes in the pot. Add the chicken and turn the pieces to coat them in the sauce. 2. Cover and turn the dial to Slow Cook, cook on low for 6 to 8 hours, until the chicken is tender. 3. Spoon over steamed rice and garnish with the scallions and sesame seeds.

Per Serving: Calories 707; Fat 24.25g; Sodium 1119mg; Carbs 68.41g; Fiber 2.1g; Sugar 25.97g; Protein 51.99g

Chapter 6 Beef, Pork and Lamb

Apricot and Cube Steaks Stew

Prep Time: 15 minutes | Cook Time: 7-8 hours | Serves: 4

1-pound cube steak
½ teaspoon salt
⅛ teaspoon pepper
¼ cup flour
1 teaspoon paprika

1 tablespoon oil
1 tablespoon butter
1 onion, chopped
½ cup beef broth
⅓ cup apricot preserves

1. Cut steak into small pieces. On shallow bowl, combine the salt, pepper, flour, and paprika; stir to mix well. Dredge steaks in this mixture. 2. Add oil and butter to the pot. Turn dial to Sear/Sauté, set temperature to LO, and press START/STOP to begin cooking. Once the butter is melted, add steaks to the pot. Brown steaks on both sides, turning once, about 3–4 minutes. 3. Add onion, apricot preserves and beef broth to the pot. Turn the heat to high, cook and stir to loosen drippings. Press START/STOP to turn off the Sear/Sauté function. 4. Cover and turn the dial to Slow Cook, cook on low for 7–8 hours or until meat is very tender. Serve meat with sauce.

Per Serving: Calories 258; Fat 9.38g; Sodium 450mg; Carbs 18.3g; Fiber 1.7g; Sugar 7.06g; Protein 24.78g

Pork, Beans and Meatballs

Prep Time: 15 minutes | Cook Time: 7-8 hours | Serves: 5

1 tablespoon olive oil
1 onion, chopped
2 cloves garlic, minced
½ cup ketchup
2 tablespoons brown sugar

2 tablespoons mustard
1 (15-ounce) can kidney beans
1 (15-ounce) can pork and beans
12 porcupine meatballs

1. Add the olive oil to the pot. Turn dial to Sear/Sauté, set temperature to LO, and press START/STOP to begin cooking. Once the oil is hot, add onion and garlic; cook and stir until tender, about 5 minutes. 2. Add ketchup, brown sugar, and mustard and bring to a simmer. Press START/STOP to turn off the Sear/Sauté function. 3. Drain kidney beans and add with pork and beans to the pot, stir to mix well. 4. Prepare Porcupine Meatballs and freeze all but 12 of them. Brown the 12 meatballs in the saucepan, about 4–5 minutes' total, then add to bean mixture. 5. Cover and turn the dial to Slow Cook, cook on low for 7–8 hours or until meatballs are thoroughly cooked and tender. Serve immediately.

Per Serving: Calories 258; Fat 16.05g; Sodium 589mg; Carbs 21.19g; Fiber 2.9g; Sugar 11.24g; Protein 9.51g

Slow–Cooker BBQ Pork

Prep Time: 15 minutes | Cook Time: 8½-10½ hours | Serves: 4

1 onion, chopped
2 cloves garlic, minced
1 jalapeño pepper, minced
½ cup taco sauce
¼ cup barbecue sauce

1 tablespoon chili powder
1¼-pound boneless pork loin roast
½ teaspoon salt
⅛ teaspoon cayenne pepper

1. Add all ingredients to the pot. Cover and turn the dial to Slow Cook, cook on low heat for 8–10 hours or until pork is very tender. 2. Remove pork and shred with 2 forks; return to the pot and cook on high for another 30 minutes. Serve over rice, or with warmed corn or flour tortillas and guacamole.

Per Serving: Calories 288; Fat 9.07g; Sodium 722mg; Carbs 14.01g; Fiber 2g; Sugar 8.71g; Protein 36.16g

Creamy Mustard Pork Loin Chops

Prep Time: 15 minutes | Cook Time: 7½-8½ hours | Serves: 4

4 boneless pork loin chops
½ teaspoon salt
⅛ teaspoon white pepper
1 tablespoon olive oil
1 onion, sliced
2 tablespoons grainy mustard

¾ cup chicken stock
1 tablespoon prepared horseradish
2 tablespoons cornstarch
½ cup sour cream
2 tablespoons Dijon mustard

1. Sprinkle the pork chops with salt and pepper. 2. Add olive oil to the pot. Turn dial to Sear/Sauté, set temperature to HI, and press START/STOP to begin cooking. Once the oil is hot, add chops to the pot; turning once, cook for about 4–6 minutes. Press START/STOP to turn off the Sear/Sauté function. Transfer to a bowl. 3. Place onions in the bottom of the pot. Add a layer of pork chops, then spread some of the grainy mustard over. Repeat, using the rest of the pork chops and the mustard. 4. Add stock to the pot. Cover and turn the dial to Slow Cook, cook on low for 7–8 hours or until chops are tender and register 155°F. 5. Remove chops from pot and cover to keep warm. Mix together the horseradish, cornstarch, sour cream, and Dijon mustard in a small bowl. Pour into pot and stir well. 6. Return chops to pot, cover, and cook on high for 30 minutes until sauce is thickened. Serve immediately.

Per Serving: Calories 348; Fat 13.84g; Sodium 657mg; Carbs 8.87g; Fiber 0.8g; Sugar 1.31g; Protein 44.27g

Ham, Peas and Cheese Potatoes

Prep Time: 15 minutes | Cook Time: 9-10 hours | Serves: 6

½ (32-ounce) package frozen straight cut French fry potatoes
1 onion, chopped
2 cloves garlic, minced
1¼ cups cubed ham
1 cup shredded Swiss cheese

1 (10-ounce) can cream of potato soup
½ cup ricotta cheese
⅛ teaspoon pepper
½ teaspoon dried marjoram
1½ cups frozen baby peas, thawed
¼ cup grated Parmesan cheese

1. Add potatoes, onions, garlic, ham, and Swiss cheese to the pot, stir to mix well. In a medium bowl, combine together the soup, cheese, pepper, and marjoram. Pour over potato mixture. 2. Cover and turn the dial to Slow Cook, cook on low for 8–9 hours or until potatoes are tender. Stir in peas and Parmesan cheese. 3. Cover and cook on high for 30–40 minutes or until peas are hot. Serve immediately.

Per Serving: Calories 312; Fat 15.25g; Sodium 362mg; Carbs 22.12g; Fiber 3.5g; Sugar 1.23g; Protein 21.8g

Curried Sausage with Sweet Potato & Apple

Prep Time: 15 minutes | Cook Time: 9-10 hours | Serves: 5

1 pound sweet Italian sausage links
1 tablespoon butter
1 onion, chopped
2 cloves garlic, minced
2 tablespoons flour
½ teaspoon salt
⅛ teaspoon pepper

2 teaspoons curry powder
¼ cup brown sugar
½ cup chicken stock
½ cup apple cider
2 sweet potatoes, peeled
2 apples, peeled and sliced
2 tablespoons brown sugar

1. Add sausage to the pot, turn dial to Sear/Sauté, set temperature to LO, and press START/STOP to begin cooking. Cook sausage until almost done; remove from the pot. 2. Add butter to drippings remaining in the pot. Add onions and garlic; cook and stir until tender, about 6 minutes. 3. Add flour, salt, pepper, and curry powder; cook and stir until bubbly. Add ¼ cup brown sugar, then stir in chicken stock and cider. Cook and stir until thickened. Press START/STOP to turn off the Sear/Sauté function. Transfer to a bowl and set aside. 4. Slice sweet potatoes into ⅛-inch thick rounds. Slice the sausage into 1-inch chunks. 5. Layer sweet potatoes, apples, sausage pieces, and onion mixture in the pot. Top with 2 tablespoons brown sugar. 6. Cover and turn the dial to Slow Cook, cook on low for 9–10 hours or until sweet potatoes are tender. Serve immediately.

Per Serving: Calories 337; Fat 10.59g; Sodium 837mg; Carbs 45.45g; Fiber 4.3g; Sugar 27.34g; Protein 17.08g

Lamb and Parsnips Stew

Prep Time: 15 minutes | Cook Time: 8 hours | Serves: 2

12 ounces boneless lamb shoulder or stew meat, cut into 1-inch pieces
⅛ teaspoon sea salt
Freshly ground black pepper
1 cup diced and peeled parsnips
1 cup diced and peeled potatoes

½ cup diced onions
1 tablespoon minced garlic
1 cup low-sodium beef broth
½ cup dark beer, such as Guinness Stout
½ tablespoon tomato paste

1. Season the lamb with the salt and black pepper. Place the lamb, potatoes, parsnips, onions, and garlic in the pot. 2. In a small bowl, mix together the beef broth, beer, and tomato paste. Pour this over the lamb and vegetables. 3. Cover and turn the dial to Slow Cook, cook on low for 8 hours.

Per Serving: Calories 469; Fat 12.26g; Sodium 313mg; Carbs 48.77g; Fiber 6.2g; Sugar 12.42g; Protein 43.12g

Juicy Pulled Pork Tortillas

Prep Time: 15 minutes | Cook Time: 8-10 hours | Serves: 6

For the Pork Roast:
2 pounds pork butt roast with bone
2 tablespoons achiote paste
½ cup orange juice
¼ cup lime juice
1 tablespoon Mexican oregano
1 teaspoon ground cumin
1 teaspoon smoked paprika
1 teaspoon chili powder

1 teaspoon ground coriander
1 teaspoon chopped garlic
½ teaspoon ground cinnamon
½ teaspoon ground allspice
Pinch salt
Pinch freshly ground black pepper
12 corn tortillas

For the Relish:
½ cup grated or finely chopped radishes
¼ cup minced red onion
1 seeded and minced habanero chile pepper
¼ cup orange juice

2 tablespoons lime juice
2 tablespoons water
¼ teaspoon kosher salt
¼ cup chopped cilantro

The Night Before: 1. Poke holes all over the pork with a fork. Rub the achiote paste all over the meat. Set aside. 2. Combine the orange juice and lime juice in a large bowl. Then add in the cumin, paprika, chili powder, cinnamon, coriander, garlic, allspice, salt, and pepper. 3. Submerge the pork in the mixture, cover, and refrigerate overnight.

In the Morning: 1. Add the pork and its overnight marinade to the pot. 2. Cover with the lid and turn the dial to Slow Cook, cook on low for 8 to 10 hours. The longer it cooks, the more tender it will be. 3. During the last hour of cooking, mix together all of the ingredients for the relish in a medium bowl. Let stand for at least 10 minute to allow the flavors to blend. 4. When the cooking is over, open the lid and shred the pork with two forks. 5. To serve, spoon the contents of the pot into tortillas, and top with the relish.

Per Serving: Calories 467; Fat 17.35g; Sodium 422mg; Carbs 31.26g; Fiber 4.6g; Sugar 5.63g; Protein 45.92g

Lamb & Rice Stew

Prep Time: 15 minutes | Cook Time: 8 hours | Serves: 2

1 teaspoon extra-virgin olive oil
½ cup brown rice
1 cup low-sodium chicken broth or water
1 scallion, white and green parts, sliced thin on a bias
2 tablespoons low-sodium soy sauce

2 tablespoons honey
1 tablespoon freshly squeezed lime juice
Pinch red pepper flakes
12 ounces boneless lamb shoulder, cut into 1-inch cubes

1. Grease the inside of the pot with the olive oil. 2. Place the brown rice, broth, and scallion to the pot. Stir to mix the ingredients and make sure the rice is submerged in the liquid. 3. Mix together the soy sauce, lime juice, honey, and red pepper flakes in a big bowl. Then, add the lamb cubes and toss to coat them in this mixture. 4. Place the lamb over the rice in the pot. 5. Cover and turn the dial to Slow Cook, cook on low for 8 hours.

Per Serving: Calories 546; Fat 17.17g; Sodium 695mg; Carbs 58.7g; Fiber 2.2g; Sugar 19.22g; Protein 41.4g

Lime Steak Fajitas

Prep Time: 15 minutes | Cook Time: 6-8 hours | Serves: 2

1 tablespoon freshly squeezed lime juice
1 tablespoon minced garlic
2 tablespoons minced chipotles in adobo
1 tablespoon extra-virgin olive oil
⅛ teaspoon sea salt
12 ounces skirt steak, sliced thin

2 bell peppers, assorted colors, cored and cut into thin strips
½ onion, halved and cut into thin half circles
4 corn tortillas
1 small avocado, sliced, for garnish

1. Combine the lime juice, garlic, chipotles, olive oil, and salt in a small bowl, stir to mix well. Add the skirt steak to the bowl and toss to thoroughly coat the meat. Marinate in the refrigerator if you desired. 2. Add the steak, peppers, and onions to the pot. 3. Cover and turn the dial to Slow Cook, cook on low heat for 6 to 8 hours. The vegetables and meat will be very tender. 4. Serve in warmed corn tortillas and garnished with the avocado slices.

Per Serving: Calories 677; Fat 36.49g; Sodium 1058mg; Carbs 39.87g; Fiber 11.5g; Sugar 5.72g; Protein 53.62g

Savory Pork Ribs with Lime Tomato Sauce

Prep Time: 15 minutes | Cook Time: 6 hours | Serves: 6

1½ pounds tomatillos with husks removed or 1 (28-ounce) can tomatillos, cut into bite-size pieces
¼ cup diced fire-roasted poblano chiles
1 medium onion, chopped
2 serrano chiles, seeded and chopped
2 teaspoons honey
4 garlic cloves, minced

1 teaspoon ground coriander
½ teaspoon ground cumin
½ teaspoon sea salt
1 tablespoon Fajita seasoning mix
2½ to 3 pounds pork loin back ribs
½ cup chopped fresh cilantro
2 tablespoons fresh lime juice

1. Mix together the tomatillos, poblanos, onion, serranos, garlic, coriander, honey, cumin, and salt in a blender. Pulse until smooth. 2. Rub all over the ribs with the fajita seasoning. 3. Add the ribs and tomatillo mixture to the pot. Cover and turn the dial to Slow Cook, cook on low for 6 hours or on high for 3 hours. 4. Remove the ribs from the pot and broil them under the highest heat until they begin to brown, about 10 minutes. Watch them carefully. 5. Skim any fat from the sauce in the pot. 6. In a medium saucepan over medium heat, simmer the sauce from the pot for 10 minutes to thicken it. 7. Stir the cilantro and lime juice into the sauce and serve it with the ribs.
Per Serving: Calories 428; Fat 17.28g; Sodium 413mg; Carbs 15.75g; Fiber 4.5g; Sugar 9.42g; Protein 51.09g

Spiced Pork Roast

Prep Time: 15 minutes | Cook Time: 8 hours | Serves: 6

2 tablespoons packed brown sugar
1½ tablespoons chipotle powder
2 teaspoons sea salt
2 teaspoons chili powder
1½ teaspoons unsweetened cocoa powder
1 teaspoon ground cumin
1 teaspoon smoked paprika
1 teaspoon dried Mexican oregano

1 teaspoon garlic powder
½ teaspoon ground roasted cinnamon
½ teaspoon freshly ground black pepper
2 pounds sirloin tip pork roast or similar quality pork roast
2 tablespoons olive oil
½ cup vegetable stock

The Night Before: 1. In a big bowl, mix together all the ingredients except the pork roast, olive oil, and vegetable stock. 2. Rub the spice mixture and the olive oil all over the roast. 3. Cover the roast tightly with plastic wrap and refrigerate it overnight.
In the Morning: 1. Pour the vegetable stock into the pot, add the roast, cover and turn the dial to Slow Cook, cook on low for 8 hours or on high for 4 hours, until the roast is fork tender. 2. Turn off the heat and let the roast stand for 10 minutes before serving.
Per Serving: Calories 410; Fat 29.07g; Sodium 892mg; Carbs 4.4g; Fiber 0.9g; Sugar 2.75g; Protein 33.17g

Pork Loin and White Cabbage Soup

Prep Time: 15 minutes | Cook Time: 7-8 hours | Serves: 6

½ tbsp. of olive oil
½ red onion, chopped
1 garlic cloves, minced
6oz of lean pork loin
½ cup of low-sodium chicken stock

1 cup of water
½ tbsp. of allspice
½ cup of white cabbage, sliced
½ tsp. of black pepper

1. Trim the fat from the pork loin meat and slice into 1-inch thick slices. 2. Add oil to the pot. Turn dial to Sear/Sauté, set temperature to LO, and press START/STOP to begin cooking. When the oil is hot, add the garlic and onion and sauté for 5 minutes. 3. Add the pork to the pot and cook for 7-8 minutes to brown. Press START/STOP to turn off the Sear/Sauté function. 4. Pour the stock and water into the pot. Add in the allspice to season. Add the in sliced cabbage and stir the pot well. 5. Cover and turn the dial to Slow Cook, cook on Low heat for 7-8 hours until the pork is very soft. 6. Sprinkle with the black pepper. Serve.

Per Serving: Calories 80; Fat 4g; Sodium 26mg; Carbs 2.33g; Fiber 0.5g; Sugar 0.71g; Protein 8.57g

Cheesy Steak and Pasta Soup

Prep Time: 15 minutes | Cook Time: 8½ hours | Serves: 8

1 (14.5-ounce) can no-salt-added diced tomatoes with green chiles
1 (16-ounce) jar salsa
1 (16-ounce) package frozen corn
1 cup pre-chopped white onion
1 tablespoon jarred minced garlic
1 (15-ounce) can no-salt-added black beans, drained and rinsed

2 pounds cubed sirloin tip steak
1 tablespoon chili powder
4 cups beef stock or store-bought beef stock
1 (16-ounce) package uncooked gemelli or mostaccioli pasta
1 cup sour cream
2 cups shredded Colby cheese

1. Add the tomatoes with their juices, salsa, black beans, corn, onion, garlic, chili powder, steak, and stock to the pot, stir well. 2. Cover and turn the dial to Slow Cook, cook on Low heat for 8 hours, or until the beef is tender. Turn the pot to High. 3. Stir in the pasta, sour cream, and cheese. Cover with the lid and cook for 20 to 30 minutes, or until the pasta is tender. 4. Store leftovers covered in the refrigerator for up to 4 days or freeze for up to 3 months.

Per Serving: Calories 459; Fat 22.36g; Sodium 1298mg; Carbs 43.24g; Fiber 7.7g; Sugar 10.75g; Protein 25.1g

Beef Meatloaf with Vegetables

Prep Time: 15 minutes | Cook Time: 8-9 hours | Serves: 6

Unsalted butter, for greasing
½ cup panko bread crumbs
½ cup grated Parmesan cheese
½ teaspoon garlic salt
2 large eggs
¼ cup whole milk

¼ cup ketchup
2 tablespoons Dijon mustard
1 teaspoon dried marjoram leaves
2 pounds 93% lean ground beef
1-pound baby red potatoes
1 (16-ounce) bag baby carrots

1. Grease the pot thoroughly with butter. 2. Add the bread crumbs, cheese, eggs, milk, garlic salt, ketchup, mustard, and marjoram to the pot and mix well. Add the ground beef and mix gently. 3. Form the meat mixture into a 5-by-9-inch loaf in the center of the pot. Surround the meat loaf with the potatoes and carrots. 4. Cover and turn the dial to Slow Cook, cook on Low for 8 to 9 hours, or until the vegetables are tender and the meat loaf registers 160°F on a food thermometer. 5. Carefully remove the vegetables from around the meat loaf and place on a serving platter. Using two large spatulas, remove the meat loaf from the pot and place on the platter. Cover with foil and let stand for 10 minutes before slicing to serve. 6. Store leftovers covered in the refrigerator for up to 4 days or freeze for up to 3 months.
Per Serving: Calories 467; Fat 21.95g; Sodium 427mg; Carbs 19.45g; Fiber 1.7g; Sugar 4.74g; Protein 45.85g

Cheese Lamb Burritos

Prep Time: 15 minutes | Cook Time: 5-6 hours | Serves: 10

1 (3-pound) boneless lamb shoulder, fat trimmed
2 teaspoons ground cumin
½ teaspoon salt
⅛ teaspoon cayenne pepper
2 cups prechopped yellow onion

2 tablespoons jarred minced garlic
1 (8-ounce) package sliced button mushrooms
1 (4-ounce) can diced green chiles, with juices
10 to 12 (10-inch) flour tortillas
2 cups shredded Pepper Jack cheese

1. Rub the lamb with the cumin, salt, and cayenne pepper. 2. Add the mushrooms, onion, garlic, and chiles with their juices to the pot, stir well. Top with the lamb. 3. Cover and turn the dial to Slow Cook, cook on Low for 5 to 6 hours, or until the lamb is very tender. Using two forks, shred the lamb in the pot and stir. 4. To assemble the burritos, layer the tortillas with cheese and top with the lamb mixture. Fold burrito-style and serve. 5. Store leftovers covered in the refrigerator for up to 4 days or freeze for up to 3 months.
Per Serving: Calories 463; Fat 23.13g; Sodium 720mg; Carbs 26.85g; Fiber 1.8g; Sugar 2.49g; Protein 36.54g

Italian Beef Roast with White Potatoes

Prep Time: 15 minutes | Cook Time: 8 hours | Serves: 8

1 (3-pound) beef chuck roast, trimmed and halved crosswise
4 garlic cloves, cut into slivers (4 slivers per clove), divided
1 teaspoon coarse sea salt
1 teaspoon freshly ground black pepper

1 tablespoon extra-virgin olive oil
1½ pounds small white potatoes
1 large yellow onion, cut into 8 wedges
1 (28-ounce) can whole tomatoes in purée
2 teaspoons dried Italian seasoning

1. Cut 4 slits in each of the beef roast halves using a sharp paring knife. Stuff each slit with a garlic sliver. Season with salt and pepper. 2. Add the olive oil to the pot. Turn dial to Sear/Sauté, set temperature to LO, and press START/STOP to begin cooking. Once the olive oil is hot, add the beef and brown on all sides for about 10 minutes total. Press START/STOP to turn off the Sear/Sauté function. Transfer the beef to a bowl. 3. Place the potatoes and onion in the bottom of the pot. Place the beef, fat-side up, on the vegetables. Pour the tomatoes over all, and sprinkle with the Italian seasoning and the remaining 8 garlic slivers. 4. Cover and turn the dial to Slow Cook, cook on low for 8 hours, until the meat is fork-tender. 5. Transfer the meat to a cutting board. Thinly slice and discard any fat or gristle. 6. Skim the fat from the top of the sauce remaining in the pot. 7. Serve hot, dividing the beef and vegetables among 8 bowls and generously spooning the sauce over the top.
Per Serving: Calories 240; Fat 8.71g; Sodium 547mg; Carbs 18.57g; Fiber 4.2g; Sugar 4.08g; Protein 22.74g

Beef Brisket in Barbecue Sauce

Prep Time: 15 minutes | Cook Time: 8-10 hours | Serves: 8

1 (3- to 4-pound) beef brisket
1 teaspoon sea salt
¼ teaspoon freshly ground black pepper
1 tablespoon extra-virgin olive oil

¼ cup water
1 teaspoon liquid smoke (optional)
¼ cup Sriracha
1 cup barbecue sauce (or store-bought gluten-free)

1. Sprinkle the brisket with the salt and pepper. 2. Add the olive oil to the pot. Turn dial to Sear/Sauté, set temperature to LO, and press START/STOP to begin cooking. Once hot, add the brisket and brown on all sides, flipping the beef frequently, for about 10 minutes total. 3. Add the water to the pot. Scraping any browned bits and drippings from the bottom of the pot with a spatula or wooden spoon. 4. Mix together the liquid smoke (if using), Sriracha, and barbecue sauce in a small bowl. Pour the mixture over the beef. 5. Cover and turn the dial to Slow Cook, cook on low for 8 to 10 hours, or until the beef is very tender. 6. You can slice or shred this beef before serving. Store the leftovers in an airtight container in the refrigerator up to 4 days.
Per Serving: Calories 464; Fat 30.56g; Sodium 1245mg; Carbs 15.4g; Fiber 0.5g; Sugar 12.2g; Protein 29.54g

Sweet & Sour Beef Short Ribs

Prep Time: 15 minutes | Cook Time: 8 hours | Serves: 4

1 yellow onion, cut crosswise into thick rings
4 pounds bone-in beef short ribs
1 cup beef broth
1 cup ketchup

¼ cup mustard
¼ cup apple cider vinegar
2 tablespoons brown sugar
1 teaspoon liquid smoke (optional)

1. Place the onion in the bottom of the pot. Top with the short ribs. 2. Mix together the broth, ketchup, brown sugar, mustard, vinegar, and liquid smoke (if using) in a small bowl. Pour the mixture over the ribs. 3. Cover and turn the dial to Slow Cook, cook on low for 8 hours, or until the beef is very tender. 4. Serve with the liquid in the pot.

Per Serving: Calories 944; Fat 53.96g; Sodium 1241mg; Carbs 27.35g; Fiber 1.6g; Sugar 19.88g; Protein 90.05g

Horseradish–Braised Short Ribs with Vegetables

Prep Time: 15 minutes | Cook Time: 8 hours | Serves: 10

2 slices bacon
6 pounds bone-in beef short ribs
4 cups bone broth (or store-bought) or beef broth, divided
1 yellow onion, chopped
2 cups fresh or frozen pearl onions, peeled
3 cups baby carrots

1 (8-ounce) package button mushrooms, halved
3 tablespoons grated fresh horseradish
1 teaspoon chopped fresh thyme
½ teaspoon sea salt
½ teaspoon freshly ground black pepper
3 tablespoons cornstarch

1. Turn dial to Sear/Sauté, set temperature to LO, add bacon to the pot and press START/STOP to begin cooking. Flip frequently and cook for 7 to 10 minutes, until brown and crispy. 2. Drain the bacon on paper towels, leaving the bacon fat in the pot; then crumble it. 3. Place the short ribs in the pot in batches; brown them on all sides, turning frequently, for 5 to 7 minutes. Drain the fat from the pot. 4. Add 1 cup of broth to the pot and bring to a boil, scraping the browned bits from the bottom of the pot. Transfer this to a large bowl. 5. Place the cooked bacon, browned short ribs, carrots, yellow onion, mushrooms, pearl onions, thyme, horseradish, salt, and pepper in the pot. Stir to combine. 6. Add the remaining 3 cups of broth and the cornstarch to the deglazing liquid in the large bowl. Whisk it together. Pour the broth mixture into the pot. 7. Cover and turn the dial to Slow Cook, cook on low for 8 hours, until the ribs are very tender. Serve the ribs with the vegetables.

Per Serving: Calories 593; Fat 36.2g; Sodium 654mg; Carbs 12.46g; Fiber 2.5g; Sugar 4.56g; Protein 55.32g

Spicy Beef and Brown Rice Casserole

Prep Time: 15 minutes | Cook Time: 7-8 hours | Serves: 5

¾ pound ground beef
1 onion, chopped
2 cloves garlic, minced
1 cup long-grain brown rice
1 cup beef stock
½ cup water
2 teaspoons chili powder

1 green bell pepper, chopped
1 jalapeño pepper, minced
1 (8-ounce) can tomato sauce
2 tablespoons taco sauce
¼ teaspoon pepper
½ cup shredded Colby cheese

1. Add ground beef, onion and garlic to the pot. Turn the dial to Sear/Sauté, set the temperature to LO, and press START/STOP to begin cooking. Cook until beef is browned. Add rice, bell peppers, and jalapeño to the pot. 2. Then, pour stock, water, chili powder, tomato sauce, pepper, and taco sauce into the pot and bring to a simmer, scraping up pan drippings. 3. Press START/STOP to turn off the Sear/Sauté function. Cover and turn the dial to Slow Cook, cook on low heat for 7–8 hours or until rice is tender. 4. Sprinkle with cheese, cover and let stand for 10 minutes, serve immediately.
Per Serving: Calories 399; Fat 16.72g; Sodium 363mg; Carbs 36.55g; Fiber 3.4g; Sugar 4.21g; Protein 25.56g

Beef and Beans in Barbecue Sauce

Prep Time: 15 minutes | Cook Time: 8½-9½ hours | Serves: 5

¾ pound 80% lean ground beef
1 onion, chopped
3 cloves garlic, minced
2 (16-ounce) cans baked beans, drained
1 (15-ounce) can black beans, drained

¼ cup brown sugar
2 tablespoons apple cider vinegar
⅓ cup ketchup
⅓ cup barbecue sauce

1. Add ground beef to the pot, turn the dial to Sear/Sauté, set temperature to LO, and press START/STOP to begin cooking. Stir to break up meat. Press START/STOP to turn off the Sear/Sauté function. 2. Add all the remaining ingredients and stir gently. Cover and turn the dial to Slow Cook, cook on low for 8–9 hours. 3. If sauce needs thickening, remove cover and cook on high for 20–30 minutes.
Per Serving: Calories 288; Fat 8.55g; Sodium 387mg; Carbs 33.3g; Fiber 4g; Sugar 22.69g; Protein 20.82g

Korean Short Ribs and Carrots Stew

Prep Time: 15 minutes | Cook Time: 8 hours | Serves: 4

2 tablespoons low-sodium soy sauce
2 tablespoons fish sauce
2 tablespoons rice wine vinegar
1 to 2 teaspoons Sriracha
1 teaspoon toasted sesame oil
2 teaspoons minced garlic
2 teaspoons minced fresh ginger
2 pounds bone-in Korean-cut short ribs, trimmed of

fat
4 carrots, cut into 2-inch pieces
3 cups low-sodium beef broth
2 tablespoons cornstarch
3 tablespoons water
1 scallion, white and green parts, thinly sliced, for garnish

1. Mix together the soy sauce, fish sauce, Sriracha, vinegar, garlic, sesame oil, and ginger in a small bowl. Spread this mixture onto the short ribs to coat thoroughly. 2. Place the carrots in the pot. Top with the short ribs. Pour in the beef broth. 3. Cover and turn the dial to Slow Cook, cook on low for 8 hours, or until the ribs are very tender. 4. Add the cornstarch and water to a small bowl and blend well. Stir this mixture into the pot. Cover and cook on high heat for 10 minutes to thicken the sauce. 5. Garnish the short ribs with the scallions and serve.

Per Serving: Calories 728; Fat 48.76g; Sodium 1208mg; Carbs 27.12g; Fiber 1.9g; Sugar 3.74g; Protein 48.78g

Garlicky Beef Brisket with Onions

Prep Time: 15 minutes | Cook Time: 7-8 hours | Serves: 8

3 large yellow onions, thinly sliced
5 garlic cloves, minced
1 (4-pound) beef brisket
Coarse sea salt

Freshly ground black pepper
2 tablespoons extra-virgin olive oil
2 cups beef broth
2 tablespoons chopped fresh parsley, for serving

1. Season the brisket with salt and pepper. 2. Add the olive oil to the pot. Turn dial to Sear/Sauté, set temperature to LO, and press START/STOP to begin cooking. 3. Once hot, add the brisket, fat-side down, and brown it for 5 minutes. Then turn and brown on the second side for another 5 minutes. Press START/STOP to turn off the Sear/Sauté function. Transfer to a bowl. 4. Add the onions and garlic to the pot. Stir to combine. Place the brisket, fat-side up, in the pot. 5. Add the broth to the pot. 6. Cover and turn the dial to Slow Cook, cook on low for 7 to 8 hours, or until the brisket is fork-tender. 7. Remove the brisket to a cutting board and thinly slice across the grain. 8. Skim the excess fat off the top of the liquid remaining in the pot and discard it. Serve the sliced beef with the onion and some cooking liquid, and sprinkle with the parsley.

Per Serving: Calories 516; Fat 39.55g; Sodium 1092mg; Carbs 3.52g; Fiber 0.7g; Sugar 1.36g; Protein 34.32g

Chapter 7 Desserts

Caramel Apple Oats Crumble

Prep Time: 15 minutes | Cook Time: 6-7 hours | Serves: 8

¼ cup butter

½ cup chopped pecans

1 cup rolled oats

½ cup brown sugar

1 teaspoon cinnamon

⅛ teaspoon cardamom

½ teaspoon salt

2 cups granola cereal

4 cups peeled apple slices

14 unwrapped caramels, chopped

3 tablespoons flour

¼ cup apple juice

1. Add butter to the pot, turn dial to Sear/Sauté, set temperature to LO, and press START/STOP to begin cooking. Once the butter is melted, add pecans and rolled oats; cook and stir until toasted and fragrant. Stir in brown sugar, cinnamon, cardamom, and salt. 2. Add granola cereal; stir and press START/STOP to turn off the Sear/Sauté function. Transfer the mixture to a bowl. 3. Clean and dry the pot. Spray the pot with nonstick cooking spray. Place apple slices and chopped caramels in it. Sprinkle with flour and top with apple juice. Top with granola mixture. 4. Cover and turn the dial to Slow Cook, cook on low for 6–7 hours or until apples are tender and topping is set. Serve with ice cream or whipped cream.

Per Serving: Calories 330; Fat 13.52g; Sodium 210mg; Carbs 55.3g; Fiber 5.9g; Sugar 32.7g; Protein 4.85g

Cherry–Oats Cobbler

Prep Time: 15 minutes | Cook Time: 5-6 hours | Serves: 6

1 (15-ounce) can sour pie cherries

¾ cup sugar

3 tablespoons flour

1 cup reserved cherry juice

6 tablespoons butter

1 cup rolled oats

½ cup granola

¾ cup brown sugar

½ teaspoon salt

½ teaspoon cinnamon

1 cup flour

½ teaspoon baking soda

1. Drain the cherries, reserving juice. In large saucepan over medium heat, combine sugar and flour, using a wire whisk to mix well. 2. Add reserved cherry juice and stir. Cook until the mixture thickens and boils. Stir in cherries and remove from heat. 3. Spray the pot with nonstick cooking spray. Place cherry mixture in the pot. 4. In a skillet over medium heat, melt the butter. Add oats; cook and stir until fragrant and lightly toasted. 5. Remove from heat and add granola, brown sugar, cinnamon and salt; mix well. Stir in flour and baking soda until crumbly. 6. Sprinkle the skillet mixture over cherry mixture in the pot. Cover and turn the dial to Slow Cook, cook on low for 5–6 hours. 7. Serve immediately with ice cream or whipped cream.

Per Serving: Calories 525; Fat 19.26g; Sodium 498mg; Carbs 88.83g; Fiber 4.7g; Sugar 46.58g; Protein 7.35g

Maple Banana–Orange Sundaes

Prep Time: 15 minutes | Cook Time: 6 hours | Serves: 6

Nonstick cooking spray
4 bananas, peeled, halved crosswise, and then halved lengthwise
2 tablespoons chopped unsalted pecans
½ cup pure maple syrup

1 teaspoon rum extract
1 tablespoon unsalted butter, melted
Zest and juice of 1 orange
Pinch sea salt
6 scoops low-fat vanilla ice cream or frozen yogurt

1. Spray the pot with nonstick cooking spray. 2. Place the bananas and unsalted pecans in the bottom of the pot. 3. Mix together the maple syrup, rum extract, orange zest and juice, butter, and salt in a small bowl. Spread the syrup mixture over the bananas and pecans. 4. Cover and turn the dial to Slow Cook, cook on low for 6 hours. 5. Spoon the bananas, pecans, and syrup over the ice cream, serve.
Per Serving: Calories 186; Fat 3.36g; Sodium 111mg; Carbs 39.83g; Fiber 2.9g; Sugar 27.63g; Protein 1.63g

Dried Fruits and Rice Pudding

Prep Time: 15 minutes | Cook Time: 8 hours | Serves: 6

⅔ cup uncooked brown rice
½ cup dried fruit of your choice, such as raisins, cranberries, apples, or a mixture
1 (13-ounce) can light coconut milk
1½ cups skim milk

¼ cup honey
1 teaspoon pure vanilla extract
1 teaspoon ground cinnamon
¼ teaspoon ground nutmeg
Pinch sea salt

1. Combine all the ingredients in the pot. 2. Cover and turn the dial to Slow Cook, cook on low for 8 hours.
Per Serving: Calories 316; Fat 16.2g; Sodium 136mg; Carbs 40.59g; Fiber 2.5g; Sugar 22.81g; Protein 5.15g

Maple Hot Chocolate

Prep Time: 15 minutes | Cook Time: 6 hours | Serves: 6

6 ounces bittersweet chocolate, chopped
3 cups skim milk
¼ cup pure maple syrup
½ teaspoon pure vanilla extract

¼ teaspoon ground cinnamon
Pinch sea salt
Pinch cayenne pepper

1. Combine all the ingredients in the pot. 2. Cover and turn the dial to Slow Cook, cook on low, whisking occasionally as the chocolate melts, for 6 hours. 3. Serve right away or reduce the heat to keep warm to serve throughout the day.
Per Serving: Calories 194; Fat 0.46g; Sodium 171mg; Carbs 43.35g; Fiber 0.8g; Sugar 37.75g; Protein 4.49g

Toffee Peach Crumble

Prep Time: 15 minutes | Cook Time: 6 hours | Serves: 6

6 peaches, peeled and sliced
1 tablespoon lemon juice
½ teaspoon cinnamon
¼ cup caramel ice cream topping
1 cup rolled oats
⅔ cup brown sugar

½ cup flour
½ teaspoon salt
½ teaspoon cinnamon
¼ cup butter, melted
1 cup granola
½ cup crushed toffee

1. Spray the pot with nonstick cooking spray. Place peaches, lemon juice, and cinnamon in the pot and mix well. Drizzle with caramel ice cream topping. 2. Mix together the oatmeal, flour, brown sugar, salt, and cinnamon in a big bowl. Add melted butter; stir until crumbly. Stir in granola and toffee. 3. Sprinkle over peach mixture in the pot. Cover and turn the dial to Slow Cook, cook on low for 6 hours or until peaches are tender and topping is hot. 4. Serve with ice cream or sweetened whipped cream.

Per Serving: Calories 359; Fat 13.17g; Sodium 307mg; Carbs 62.44g; Fiber 3.6g; Sugar 39.53g; Protein 5.45g

Chocolate Cheesecake

Prep Time: 15 minutes | Cook Time: 3 hours | Serves: 10

1 (3-ounce) package cream cheese, cubed
½ cup milk
1 cup sour cream
¼ cup cocoa
1 egg

2 (8.2-ounce) packages chocolate chip muffin mix
2 tablespoons butter
½ cup brown sugar
½ cup caramel ice cream topping
½ cup water

1. In a small microwave-safe bowl, mix the cream cheese and milk. Microwave on 50 percent power for 1 minute; remove and stir. Continue microwaving for 30-second intervals until cream cheese melts; stir with a wire whisk. 2. Transfer to a large bowl, stir in sour cream, cocoa powder, and egg. Mix well. Add both packages muffin mix and stir just until combined. 3. Spray the pot with nonstick baking spray containing flour. Spread batter evenly in pot. 4. In a small saucepan, mix together the butter, brown sugar, ice cream topping, and water; heat to boiling, stirring until blended. Pour over the batter carefully in the pot. 5. Cover and turn the dial to Slow Cook, cook on high for 3 hours or until cake springs back when lightly touched. Once done, uncover the lid and top loosely with foil, and let stand for 30 minutes. 6. Gently run a sharp knife around the edges of the cake and invert over serving plate until cake drops out. If any sauce remains in pot, spoon over cake. Cool for 30–45 minutes before serving.

Per Serving: Calories 277; Fat 15.59g; Sodium 167mg; Carbs 32.41g; Fiber 0.7g; Sugar 13.19g; Protein 4.38g

Apricots Pancakes

Prep Time: 15 minutes | Cook Time: 8 minutes | Serves: 2

1 tsp vanilla extract

2 egg whites

2 tbsp of all-purpose flour

1 tbsp coconut oil

¼ cup canned apricots, sliced

1 tsp nutmeg

1. In a medium bowl, combine together all ingredients. 2. Mix well to form a thick batter. 3. Add the coconut oil to the pot. Turn dial to Sear/Sauté, set temperature to HI, and press START/STOP to begin cooking. 4. Once the oil is hot, pour half the mixture into the center of the pot to form a pancake and cook through for 3-4 minutes per side. 5. Serve with the peach slices and a dusting of nutmeg.

Per Serving: Calories 155; Fat 7.42g; Sodium 57mg; Carbs 17.18g; Fiber 1.6g; Sugar 9.24g; Protein 5.02g

Easy Blueberry Muffins

Prep Time: 15 minutes | Cook Time: 20 minutes | Serves: 4

3 egg whites

¼ cup all-purpose white flour

1 tbsp coconut flour

1 tsp of baking soda

1 tbsp nutmeg, grated

1 tsp vanilla extract

1 tsp stevia

¼ cup fresh blueberries

1. Mix all ingredients in a large mixing bowl. 2. Spray the bottom of the pot with non-stick cooking spray. Place the batter in the pot. 3. Cover and turn the dial to Bake. Set the temperature to 325°F and set the time to 20 minutes. Press START/STOP to begin cooking.

Your knife should pull out clean from the middle of the muffin once done. 4. Allow to cool on a wired rack and cut into 4 portions before serving.

Per Serving: Calories 68; Fat 0.82g; Sodium 361mg; Carbs 12.07g; Fiber 0.9g; Sugar 3.75g; Protein 3.74g

Chickpea Brownies

Prep Time: 15 minutes | Cook Time: 30 minutes | Serves: 15

1 (15-ounce) can chickpeas, drained and rinsed

3 tablespoons nut butter of choice

¾ teaspoon baking powder

2 teaspoons vanilla extract

⅛ teaspoon baking soda

¾ cup brown sugar

1 tablespoon unsweetened applesauce

¼ cup ground flaxseed meal

2¼ teaspoons cinnamon

1. Blend all of the ingredients in a food processor until very smooth. Scoop into the pot. 2. Turn the dial to Bake. Set the temperature to 350°F and set the time to 30 minutes. Press START/STOP to begin cooking. 3. Bake until the tops are medium golden brown. Allow the brownies to cool completely before cutting.

Per Serving: Calories 103; Fat 3.38g; Sodium 58mg; Carbs 16.7g; Fiber 2.4g; Sugar 11.77g; Protein 2.41g

Savory Crème Brûlée

Prep Time: 15 minutes | Cook Time: 3 hours | Serves: 4

1 cup heavy (whipping) cream
1 cup half-and-half
4 large egg yolks

½ packed cup brown sugar
1 teaspoon pure vanilla extract
4 tablespoons granulated sugar

1. Add the heavy cream, egg yolks, half-and-half, brown sugar, and vanilla extract to a bowl and mix well. Divide the mixture among 4 (8-ounce) ramekins. 2. Pour 2 cups of hot water into the pot. Gently set the ramekins in the water, making sure no water gets into the ramekins. Lay three paper towels over the top of the pot and close the lid on top of the towels. 3. Turn the dial to Slow Cook and cook on high for 3 hours. Test for doneness by jiggling one of the ramekins with a spoon. The top should be nearly set. If it is not, cover and cook for 15 minutes before checking again. 4. Using sturdy tongs, with a kitchen mitt on your other hand, carefully transfer the ramekins to a wire rack to cool for 1 hour; then transfer to the refrigerator to cool and set completely. 5. Sprinkle the top of each of the custards evenly with 1 tablespoon sugar. Use a kitchen torch to caramelize the sugar, or you can place the ramekins on a baking sheet and broil them on high for a minute or two until the sugar browns and melts. Serve right away.

Per Serving: Calories 331; Fat 16.42g; Sodium 86mg; Carbs 41.76g; Fiber 0g; Sugar 38.47g; Protein 4.85g

Lime Pots de Crème

Prep Time: 15 minutes | Cook Time: 3 hours | Serves: 6

2 tablespoons unsalted butter
4 large egg yolks
1 (14-ounce) can sweetened condensed milk
½ cup Key lime juice

2 teaspoons grated lime zest, plus more for serving
1 tablespoon tequila
Whipped cream, for serving

1. Grease 6 (4-ounce) ramekins with the butter. 2. In a medium bowl, mix together the egg yolks and the condensed milk until well blended. Add the lime zest, lime juice, and tequila, and stir until smooth and well blended. 3. Place a folded tea towel on the bottom of the pot. 4. Add the lime mixture to the ramekins and place them on the towel in the pot. 5. Carefully pour the warm water around the ramekins in the pot until it reaches halfway up the sides of the ramekins. (Make sure the water reaches no more than halfway up the sides; it will ruin the pots de crème if it splashes into the ramekins.) 6. Lay a clean kitchen towel over the top of the pot and close the lid on top of the towel. 7. Turn the dial to Slow Cook, cook on high for 3 hours, or until a food thermometer registers at least 160°F. 8. Remove the ramekins using tongs or hot pads. Let them cool on a wire rack at room temperature for an hour, and then refrigerate them for at least 3 hours. 9. Top with a dollop of whipped cream and a sprinkling of lime zest before serving.

Per Serving: Calories 118; Fat 8.59g; Sodium 54mg; Carbs 6.27g; Fiber 0.1g; Sugar 4.43g; Protein 4.38g

Fruity Wine–Poached Pears

Prep Time: 15 minutes | Cook Time: 6 hours | Serves: 6

3 cups fruity red wine, such as zinfandel
½ cup sugar
¼ cup brandy (optional)
1 orange, cut into slices

2 cinnamon sticks
8 ripe pears, peeled and cut into slices
Vanilla ice cream, for serving

1. Combine the wine, sugar, and brandy (if using) in the pot. Stir until the sugar is partially dissolved. 2. Gently stir in the sliced orange, cinnamon, and pears. 3. Cover and turn the dial to Slow Cook, cook on low for 6 hours, until the pears are very tender. 4. Transfer the pears to individual serving dishes. Serve with the vanilla ice cream.

Per Serving: Calories 164; Fat 0.82g; Sodium 27mg; Carbs 35.39g; Fiber 7.5g; Sugar 21.72g; Protein 1.74g

Mixed Berries Cobbler

Prep Time: 15 minutes | Cook Time: 6 hours | Serves: 6

8 cups fresh or frozen assorted berries, such as strawberries, blueberries, and blackberries
2 tablespoons cornstarch
1 tablespoon lemon juice

½ cup sugar
1 (16-ounce) package refrigerated biscuits
Whipped cream or vanilla ice cream, for serving

1. Add the berries, lemon juice, cornstarch, and sugar to the pot. Stir the mixture until the berries are well coated in the cornstarch. 2. Spread the biscuits over the berry mixture. 3. Cover and turn the dial to Slow Cook, cook on low for 6 hours or on high for 3 hours. 4. Serve with the whipped cream.

Per Serving: Calories 190; Fat 2.33g; Sodium 74mg; Carbs 43.84g; Fiber 5.7g; Sugar 27.97g; Protein 1.75g

Sweet Pumpkin Butter

Prep Time: 15 minutes | Cook Time: 6 hours | Serves: 8

2 (28-ounce) cans pumpkin puree
2 cups unfiltered apple cider
1½ cups brown sugar
1 teaspoon ground cinnamon

1 teaspoon ground ginger
1 teaspoon ground nutmeg
¼ teaspoon sea salt

1. Add the pumpkin puree, apple cider, cinnamon, ginger, brown sugar, nutmeg, and salt to the pot. Gently stir to mix well. 2. Cover and turn the dial to Slow Cook, cook on low for 6 hours, stirring once or twice, until it is very thick and flavorful.

Per Serving: Calories 194; Fat 0.23g; Sodium 86mg; Carbs 49.65g; Fiber 2g; Sugar 44.94g; Protein 0.88g

Classic Apple Pie Filling

Prep Time: 15 minutes | Cook Time: 6 hours | Serves: 6

8 tart apples, such as Granny Smith or Pink Lady, peeled, cored, and cut into slices
1½ teaspoons ground cinnamon
¼ teaspoon ground nutmeg

¼ teaspoon sea salt
4 tablespoons (½ stick) cold butter, cut into pieces
1 tablespoon all-purpose flour or gluten-free flour
½ cup brown sugar

1. Mix together the apples, cinnamon, butter, flour, nutmeg, salt, and brown sugar in the pot. 2. Cover and turn the dial to Slow Cook, cook on low for 6 hours, until the apples are very tender.
Per Serving: Calories 271; Fat 8.15g; Sodium 165mg; Carbs 53.07g; Fiber 6.2g; Sugar 43.03g; Protein 0.9g

Delicious Chocolate–Mint Truffles

Prep Time: 25 minutes | Cook Time: 5 minutes | Serves: 12

14 ounces semisweet chocolate, coarsely chopped
¾ cup half-and-half
½ teaspoon pure vanilla extract
1½ teaspoon peppermint extract

2 tablespoons unsalted butter, softened
¾ cup naturally unsweetened or Dutch-process cocoa powder

1. Place semisweet chocolate in a large microwave-safe bowl. 2. Microwave in four 15-second increments, stirring after each, for a total of 60 seconds. Stir until almost completely melted. Set aside. 3. Add the half-and-half to the pot, turn dial to Sear/Sauté, set temperature to LO, and press START/STOP to begin cooking. Stir occasionally, until it just begins to boil. Press START/STOP to turn off the Sear/Sauté function. Then add the vanilla and peppermint extracts. 4. Pour the mixture over the chocolate and, using a wooden spoon, gently stir in one direction. 5. Once the chocolate and cream are smooth, stir in the butter until it is combined and melted. 6. Cover with plastic wrap pressed on the top of the mixture, then let it sit at room temperature for 30 minutes. 7. After 30 minutes, place the mixture in the refrigerator until it is thick and can hold a ball shape, about 5 hours. 8. Line a baking sheet with parchment paper. Set aside. 9. Remove the mixture from the refrigerator. Place the cocoa powder in a bowl. 10. Scoop 1 teaspoon of the ganache and, using your hands, roll into a ball. Roll the ball in the cocoa powder, the place on the prepared baking sheet. 11. Serve right away or cover and store at room temperature for up to one week.
Per Serving: Calories 125; Fat 2.57g; Sodium 40mg; Carbs 26g; Fiber 2.5g; Sugar 17.26g; Protein 2.12g

Chocolate Chia Seeds Pudding with Berries

Prep Time: 15 minutes | Cook Time: 0 minutes | Serves: 4

1½ cups unsweetened vanilla almond milk
¼ cup unsweetened cocoa powder
¼ cup maple syrup (or substitute any sweetener)
½ teaspoon vanilla extract
⅓ cup chia seeds

½ cup strawberries
¼ cup blueberries
¼ cup raspberries
2 tablespoons unsweetened coconut flakes
¼ to ½ teaspoon ground cinnamon (optional)

1. Combine the almond milk, maple syrup, cocoa powder, and vanilla extract in a blender and blend until smooth. Stir in the chia seeds. 2. Gently mash the strawberries with a fork in a small bowl. Distribute the strawberry mash evenly to the bottom of 4 glass jars. 3. Pour equal portions of the milk-cocoa mixture into each of the jars and let the pudding chill in the refrigerator until it achieves a pudding like consistency, at least 3 to 5 hours and up to overnight. 4. Transfer to serving bowls and top with blueberries, raspberries, coconut flakes, and cinnamon (if using).

Per Serving: Calories 158; Fat 3.29g; Sodium 69mg; Carbs 33.56g; Fiber 4.3g; Sugar 26.04g; Protein 2.22g

Mango Wontons

Prep Time: 15 minutes | Cook Time: 20 minutes | Serves: 12

Cooking spray
12 small wonton wrappers
1 tablespoon cornstarch
½ cup water
3 cups finely chopped mango (fresh, or thawed

from frozen, no sugar added)
2 tablespoons brown sugar (not packed)
½ teaspoon cinnamon
1 tablespoon light whipped butter or buttery spread
Unsweetened coconut flakes (optional)

1. Spray a 12-cup muffin pan with nonstick cooking spray. 2. Place a wonton wrapper into each cup of the muffin pan, pressing it into the bottom and up along the sides. Transfer the muffin pan to the pot. 3. Spray the wrappers with nonstick spray. Cover and turn the dial to Bake. Set the temperature to 350°F and set the time to 8 minutes. Bake until lightly browned. 4. In the meantime, mix the cornstarch and water in a medium nonstick saucepan over medium heat. Stir to dissolve. Add the mango, brown sugar, and cinnamon. 5. Stirring often, cook until the mangoes have slightly softened and the mixture is thick and gooey, 6 to 8 minutes. 6. Remove the mango mixture from heat and stir in the butter. 7. Spoon the mango mixture into wonton cups, about 3 tablespoons each. Top with coconut flakes (if using) and serve warm.

Per Serving: Calories 133; Fat 1.06g; Sodium 202mg; Carbs 27.41g; Fiber 1.5g; Sugar 7.43g; Protein 3.63g

Nutty Cherry Bread Pudding

Prep Time: 15 minutes | Cook Time: 9 hours | Serves: 6

5 cups French bread cubes
3 eggs, beaten
1 cup heavy cream
½ cup whole milk
⅔ cup sugar
3 tablespoons butter, melted

1 teaspoon vanilla
¼ teaspoon salt
1 cup dried cherries, chopped
¾ cup chopped pecans
½ cup caramel ice cream topping

1. Place bread cubes in the pot. Turn dial to Bake, set the temperature to 300°F and set the time to 35 minutes. Press START/STOP to begin cooking. When the cooking is complete, add the cherries and pecans; mix gently. 2. In large bowl, whisk together the eggs, cream, butter, milk, sugar, vanilla, and salt. Pour into pot. Let stand for 15 minutes, pushing down on bread mixture occasionally so it absorbs the sauce. 3. Cover and turn the dial to Slow Cook, cook on high for 3 hour, then reduce the heat to low and cook for 6 hours longer until pudding is fluffy and set. 4. Spoon into dessert bowls and top with a drizzle of caramel ice cream topping.

Per Serving: Calories 692; Fat 31.65g; Sodium 917mg; Carbs 84.32g; Fiber 4.3g; Sugar 25.83g; Protein 19.73g

Delicious Peanut Butter Fondue

Prep Time: 15 minutes | Cook Time: 6 hours | Serves: 6

1 cup peanut butter
1 (14-ounce) can sweetened condensed milk
1 (13-ounce) can evaporated milk
1 cup peanut butter flavored chips

¼ cup butter
Sliced apples
Marshmallows
½ cup chopped peanuts

1. Add the peanut butter, both kinds of milk, chips, and butter to the pot; mix well. 2. Cover and turn the dial to Slow Cook, cook on low for 6 hours or until mixture is smooth, stirring once during the cooking time. 3. Arrange dippers on a platter around the fondue, and provide forks, skewers, or toothpicks. 4. Dip fruits and marshmallows into the fondue and roll into peanuts.

Per Serving: Calories 548; Fat 36g; Sodium 1236mg; Carbs 42.2g; Fiber 3.7g; Sugar 30g; Protein 16.81g

Vanilla Apricot Rice Pudding

Prep Time: 15 minutes | Cook Time: 4-5 hours | Serves: 6

1 cup medium grain white rice
1 cup sugar
¼ cup butter
¼ teaspoon salt
⅛ teaspoon cardamom
⅛ teaspoon nutmeg

2 cups apricot nectar
1 cup light cream
1 cup milk
2 teaspoons vanilla
½ cup finely chopped dried apricots
1 cup chopped canned apricots in juice, drained

1. Combine all ingredients except canned apricots in the pot. Cover and turn the dial to Slow Cook, cook on low for 2 hours, then remove lid and stir. 2. Cover and continue cooking on low for 2–3 hours longer, until rice is tender and pudding is desired thickness, stirring every 30 minutes. 3. Stir in canned apricots, cover, and cook for another 30 minutes. Serve warm or cold.

Per Serving: Calories 452; Fat 17.07g; Sodium 197mg; Carbs 70.51g; Fiber 2.9g; Sugar 41.7g; Protein 5.55g

Vanilla –Chocolate Fondue

Prep Time: 15 minutes | Cook Time: 6 hours | Serves: 8

½ cup unsalted butter, at room temperature
2 cups brown sugar
⅓ cup cocoa powder
1 cup semisweet chocolate chips
1 (14-ounce) can sweetened condensed milk

1 cup butterscotch ice cream sauce
2 teaspoons pure vanilla extract
¼ teaspoon sea salt
½ cup water

1. In an 8-cup bowl that will fit inside of the pot, combine the butter, cocoa powder, brown sugar, chocolate chips, butterscotch sauce, condensed milk, vanilla extract, and salt. 2. Place the bowl in the pot and add the water to the bottom of the pot, creating a bath around the bowl. 3. Cover and turn the dial to Slow Cook, cook on low for about 6 hours, stirring the mixture occasionally, until the sauce is smooth.

Per Serving: Calories 352; Fat 20.65g; Sodium 114mg; Carbs 38.05g; Fiber 4.6g; Sugar 28.54g; Protein 5.67g

Conclusion

As we conclude the Ninja Foodi PossibleCooker Cookbook, we celebrate the new adventure in the kitchen. The cookbook highlighted the fundamentals and recipes and empowered you to use the Ninja Foodi PossibleCooker fully.

In each dish you prepare in your kitchen, find the joy of creativity and the celebration of flavors. The Ninja Foodi PossibleCooker is your friend in the kitchen, giving you a chance to experiment with different recipes. Remember, cooking is a learning process, and the more you do it, the more you learn and perfect. Go out there and fill your kitchen with the unique aromas. Let Ninja Foodi PossibleCooker change your experience in the kitchen. Happy cooking!

Appendix 1 Measurement Conversion Chart

VOLUME EQUIVALENTS (LIQUID)

US STANDARD	US STANDARD (OUNCES)	METRIC (APPROXIMATE)
2 tablespoons	1 fl.oz	30 mL
¼ cup	2 fl.oz	60 mL
½ cup	4 fl.oz	120 mL
1 cup	8 fl.oz	240 mL
1½ cup	12 fl.oz	355 mL
2 cups or 1 pint	16 fl.oz	475 mL
4 cups or 1 quart	32 fl.oz	1 L
1 gallon	128 fl.oz	4 L

TEMPERATURES EQUIVALENTS

FAHRENHEIT (F)	CELSIUS (C) (APPROXIMATE)
225 °F	107 °C
250 °F	120 °C
275 °F	135 °C
300 °F	150 °C
325 °F	160 °C
350 °F	180 °C
375 °F	190 °C
400 °F	205 °C
425 °F	220 °C
450 °F	235 °C
475 °F	245 °C
500 °F	260 °C

VOLUME EQUIVALENTS (DRY)

US STANDARD	METRIC (APPROXIMATE)
⅛ teaspoon	0.5 mL
¼ teaspoon	1 mL
½ teaspoon	2 mL
¾ teaspoon	4 mL
1 teaspoon	5 mL
1 tablespoon	15 mL
¼ cup	59 mL
½ cup	118 mL
¾ cup	177 mL
1 cup	235 mL
2 cups	475 mL
3 cups	700 mL
4 cups	1 L

WEIGHT EQUIVALENTS

US STANDARD	METRIC (APPROXINATE)
1 ounce	28 g
2 ounces	57 g
5 ounces	142 g
10 ounces	284 g
15 ounces	425 g
16 ounces (1 pound)	455 g
1.5pounds	680 g
2pounds	907 g

Appendix 2 Recipes Index

Made in the USA
Las Vegas, NV
12 March 2024

87116772R00058